RETIREMENT
REALITY
CHECK

DISCLAIMER

This book is designed to provide readers with a general overview of financial markets and how they work. While the method of investment described in this book is believed to be effective, there is no guarantee that the method will be profitable in specific applications or not result in financial loss, given the risks involved in investing of almost any kind. It is very important to do your own analysis before making any investment based upon your own personal circumstances. This book is not designed to be a definitive investment guide or to take the place of advice from a qualified financial planner, legal advisor, or other professional. Laws and practices often vary from state to state, and if legal or other expert assistance is required, the services of a professional should be sought. While the author has made every attempt to ensure that the information contained in this book has been obtained from reliable sources, neither the publisher nor the author is responsible for any errors or omissions, or for the results obtained from the use of this information. Thus, the publisher and the author specifically disclaim any and all liability of any kind for any losses that may be sustained by the use of, or applying the methods described in, this book.

Please remember that past performance may not be indicative of future results. Different types of investments involve varying degrees of risk, and there can be no assurance that the future performance of any specific investment, investment strategy, or product, including the investments and/or investment strategies recommended or undertaken by Wealth Quarterback, LLC ("WQL"), or any noninvestment related content made reference to directly or indirectly in this book will be profitable, equal any corresponding indicated historical performance level(s), be suitable for your portfolio or individual situation, or prove successful. Due to various factors, including changing market conditions and/or applicable laws, the content may no longer be reflective of current opinions or positions. Moreover, you should not assume that any discussion or information contained in this book serves as the receipt of, or as a substitute for, personalized investment advice from WQL. To the extent that a reader has any questions regarding the applicability of any specific issue discussed above to his/her individual situation, he/she is encouraged to consult with the professional advisor of his/her choosing. WQL is neither a law firm nor a certified public accounting firm, and no portion of this book should be construed as legal or accounting advice. A copy of the WQL's current written disclosure brochure discussing our advisory services and fees is available upon request.

Securities offered through American Portfolios Financial Services, Inc., Member FINRA/SIPC. Advisory services through Wealth Quarterback, LLC (WQ). Insurance services offered through Jalinski Advisory Group, Inc., APFS, and WQ are unaffiliated entities.

While great efforts have been taken to provide accurate and current information regarding the covered material, neither Jalinski Advisory Group, Inc.; Wealth Quarterback, LLC; Financial Quarterback Books, LLC; nor American Portfolios, Inc., is responsible for any errors or omissions, or for the results obtained from the use of this information.

The name of the book is a concept and does not guarantee or imply that changes will be made to your wealth. The act of purchasing any book, course, or financial product holds no such guarantees.

The ideas, suggestions, general principles, and conclusions presented here are subject to local, state, and federal laws and regulations and revisions of same and are intended for informational purposes only. All information in this report is provided "as is," with no guarantee of completeness, accuracy, or timeliness regarding the results obtained from the use of this information. And without warranty of any kind, express or implied, including, but not limited to, warranties of performance, merchantability, and fitness for a particular purpose. Your use of this information is at your own risk.

You assume full responsibility and risk of loss resulting from the use of this information.

The stories in this book are for entertainment and not to be construed as a testimonial in any way.

RETIREMENT REALITY CHECK

HOW TO SPEND YOUR MONEY AND STILL LEAVE AN AMAZING LEGACY

JOSH JALINSKI

HarperCollins
Leadership

AN IMPRINT OF HarperCollins

Published by HarperCollins Leadership,
an imprint of HarperCollins Focus LLC.

Book design by Maria Fernandez, Neuwirth & Associates.

ISBN 978-1-4002-1215-6 (eBook)
ISBN 978-1-4002-1214-9 (TP)

Library of Congress Cataloguing-in-Publication Data

Library of Congress Control Number: 2019931172

Printed in the United States of America

19 20 21 22 LSC 10 9 8 7 6 5 4 3 2 1

CONTENTS

CONTENTS

PART III—SPEND 'TIL THE END

PART IV—LEAVE IT!

FOREWORD

The Retirement Reality Check is an in-your-face, practical guide to a better retirement. Josh Jalinski looks at how traditional financial planning wisdom has failed retirees and debunks conventional rules that are not setting you up to live your best financial life. Rule 12, "The pie is a lie," particularly resonates with me. The average financial advisor or financial magazine may tell you to diversify, according to the Modern Portfolio Theory's pie, among 60 percent stock and 40 percent bonds. Josh recommends you "consider diversifying to trading strategies, not just asset classes." This is something I do for my investors.

Broad portfolio diversification failed in 2008. I predict that in the middle of the next decade, we will enter a similar period I call "The Great Reset." This will be a reset of nearly $500 trillion in global debt and a restructuring of massively underfunded pension systems. These problems exist in almost all of the developed world, and there is a way forward, but I encourage you to advance with a plan, and this book is the perfect place to start.

RETIREMENT ISN'T HAPPENING, AND SOCIAL SECURITY ISN'T ENOUGH

I have long said I don't want to retire, but many Americans don't have that luxury. Some have to retire because of illness or because their work requires more physical ability than their age allows. Many others don't retire because they just can't afford to.

Say you want to stop working when you're 65. You're in good health, and your family tends toward long lives. You expect to reach 90, after having been retired for 25 years. Will Social Security alone be enough?

If you have spent most of your life paying as much as legally possible into the system, and you retire in 2019 at age 65, your monthly benefit will be $2,757, which jumps to $3,770 if you delay retirement until age 70. Considering how much you would have contributed over 50-plus working years, it's probably not a great return, but it's something. Yet most people get less.

A solid majority of Social Security recipients receive $2,000 a month or less, and many less than $1,000. The average benefit is $1,413, according to Social Security's latest fact sheet. If that's all you have, your retirement lifestyle is not going to be very comfortable.

Bottom line: Social Security probably won't give you much security. You need more. Josh has a great plan for making sure your retirement income is significantly higher than what Social Security will deliver.

IS THAT ALL THERE IS?

Eighty percent of you reading this book have less than $100,000 in savings. That isn't enough to survive on, much less enjoy retirement. Let's make the very aggressive assumption that you can take 5 percent a year from your savings plan. If you have $100,000, that's $5,000 yearly or about $417 a month—on top of your Social Security. And what happens if you don't have your house paid off? Or your car?

Many of our parents and grandparents had pensions and other guaranteed defined retirement benefits from the corporations they worked for. Those are increasingly an endangered species in the private sector, while 401(k)s, IRAs (Individual Retirement Accounts), and Social Security aren't giving the average person enough to retire with anything close to a comfortable lifestyle. In this essential book, Josh will show you how to create a personal pension plan.

THE INDEXING PROBLEM IN
RETIREMENT ACCOUNTS

Back-of-the-napkin math (and a rough napkin at that) says your retirement accounts are at least 50 percent invested in equity index funds. Some of you are now asking: "What's the problem? All those index funds have come back. Everybody is back to where they started. And they are cheap."

Not so fast, Jack. As I have said, bear markets that are not accompanied by a recession have V-shaped recoveries. Which is exactly what we got.

Bear markets that *are* accompanied by recession take a very long time to recover and will likely be in the 40–50 percent loss range. A 50 percent loss requires a 100 percent gain to break even. That took about five years from the bottom of the last bear market.

When the next recession and bear market hit, it will take longer to bounce back, and the recovery will be even slower than this last one. A large amount of debt slows recoveries. Very large amounts create flat economies, and we are approaching extremely large amounts in the US.

The next recession could cause a $30 trillion debt for the US government, which will soon increase to $40 trillion. This book will arm you with strategies for dealing with the upcoming market volatility.

DOUBLE PROBLEM

I speak at various investment events every year. Lack of retirement savings is by far the most common worry I hear about at those events. Sometimes it verges on panic, even among people who spent decades earning good incomes and saving all they could.

The baby boom generation that is now reaching retirement age has a double problem. First, many didn't save enough cash to support a comfortable retirement. Second, they could lose a great deal of their IRAs when the national debt forces our government to raise tax rates.

I believe we will experience The Great Reset over the coming decade. If you are in your 50s, 60s, or 70s, put a game plan in place that enables you to better navigate the period ahead. This is where Josh comes in. He delivers the Retirement Reality Check that will get you on the right track, whether you are 20 years or just a couple of years out from retirement.

—John Mauldin

PART I

START YOUR RETIREMENT REALITY CHECK

REALITY CHECK

QUIT WORRYING ABOUT YOUR MONEY. MOST RETIREMENT PLANNING ADVICE IS WRONG.

MEET KENNY

"If you lose my money, I'm going to kill you."

What would possess a 58-year-old man to say that to me? Kenny is six foot five with the build of a lumberjack. His grip nearly crushes the person on the other side of a handshake—in this instance, that was me. I was scared.

When I first met him, Kenny hated financial advisors. His first two advisors had shipwrecked his life savings.

Kenny was so mad at his previous financial advisors that he vowed never to speak to one again. He woke up in the middle of the night in cold sweats from worrying about his future. For Kenny, retirement didn't beckon; it loomed.

Sound familiar? Millions of people like Kenny, and probably you, have either been failed by the conventional approaches to financial planning or have been too confused or scared to even get involved with them.

You're not to blame, but much of conventional financial planning wisdom is flawed.

Most of what is sold as sound financial advice is either outdated or marketed as a one-size-fits-all package. It often doesn't work for people with out-of-the-ordinary circumstances or preferences.

A lot of people I see have dabbled in financial products they've seen advertised on TV or the web or heard about in books by financial gurus. These products—and yes, they're very much products, like a washing machine or a new car—range from stocks and funds to annuities to long-term-care insurance to whole life insurance to bond ladders, and more. They're all legitimate and can be used in constructing your financial plan.

But . . .

Any financial product is a tool. It can be used for either good or ill, depending on the financial plan. As I will say over and over—it's the most important thing you should take away from this book—get a plan before you get any product. *Plan and process should precede product.*

A LEGACY

This book is dedicated to my parents, Bill and Marilyn, who loved Jesus, their family, and Mickey Mouse. They left me a godly legacy of love and selfless service to others. They devoted their lives to helping others struggling with addiction and both recently passed away within six months of each other. They didn't want to worry about their money but had to due to their many disabilities. They did what normal people were supposed to do—cancel their insurance policies and buy index funds. If they would have followed some of the strategies in this book, they wouldn't have needed me to give them a job. The reason I wrote this book is because the vast majority of Middle America is misinformed, as my parents were, about money management and protective strategies for their money.

Kenny, like my parents, made bad decisions in part due to a legacy of many decades of rigid, poorly explained advice from countless personal-finance websites, newspapers, and magazines. This information only got more rigid and more poorly explained as computers took over from economists scribbling formulas on chalkboards. Poor advice also abounded with the exponential growth of financial cable networks and the financial celebrities they helped make famous.

Many of these people mean well, but those who book guests for these shows or author these stories are usually former English majors hired for their ability to craft a compelling financial piece. Or they are social media mavens who know how to generate web traffic. There's nothing wrong with this, except that they generally borrow stories from groupthink or conventional wisdom. Many times, they do not have access to cutting-edge financial information.

There's also nothing wrong with doing research online, if you keep in mind that Google isn't the internet's equivalent to the old library card catalog; it's one of the biggest businesses in the world for a reason. We like to search for free, and Google sells our data. For instance, if you type the word "annuities" into the website, a leading default you're offered is "annuities are bad," and one of the top paid websites advertised is for an advisor who famously offers lists of why annuities are bad investments. He or she pays to be at the top of the Google surf engines. It's good marketing but often misinforms.

So why read another book full of financial planning advice? This one in particular?

A HOLISTIC APPROACH

Here you'll find a holistic approach to your finances that can be easily tailored to any situation, while offering you a set of tools used to potentially generate more income from what you already have, spend your money in a way that you enjoy, and still leave a legacy for family or causes that are dear to you.

You'll find that a lot of the old, outdated rules seem perversely designed to make you suffer rather than enjoy your money throughout your life. But rules are made to be broken, given the right circumstances. My approach will give you an in-your-face look at how traditional financial planning wisdom has failed you. Here are the conventional rules that are not setting you up to live your best financial life:

1. *Save for a rainy day.* We want the shift to savings to become a joy, not drudgery.

2. *Always max out your 401(k).* This isn't terrible advice, *but sometimes it's not the best advice.* I appreciate the 401(k) as a forced-saving vehicle. But if you max out your 401(k), you're choosing to pay taxes at a future date set by the government at a future rate controlled by a future president or Congress that may believe in confiscatory taxation. Remember, a 401(k) is a promise the government makes that they won't tax you now, but *they will tax you later.*

3. *Buy term insurance instead of whole life insurance and invest the difference you pay in the stock market.* (Also known as buy term and invest the difference.) Term insurance is akin to renting your house; whole life is like buying a home in that it builds equity. Term life insurance is a temporary tool for affordable protection of your family when you are young and can't afford a good permanent life insurance policy. However, as you age, term becomes expensive when you need it most—when you're older. Your focus should be on buying cash-value life insurance over time and investing the difference.

4. *I'd rather die and "go to hell" than buy an annuity.* Annuities can be the pension you never had but always wanted.

5. *Use a Monte Carlo Simulation to test your retirement scenario.* That's one option, but we'll give you a better game plan. After all, why would you want to follow a simulation named after a casino?

6. *Make a budget and stick to it.* Sure, except when you want to buy a new car, take a vacation, or go out to dinner. We'll show you an easy way to put your savings on autopilot and have money for saving, living, and giving.

7. *Wait until you are 70½ to take any money out of your Individual Retirement Account (IRA).* That's when you're required to take some out. There are a lot of situations, as we'll see, when you should draw down this account a bit earlier.

8. *You can't do anything to prepare for a stock market meltdown.* Set up a volatility buffer to draw from when the markets get choppy, so you don't have to spend your principal in a down year.

9. *All you need in retirement is three checks: your pension, Social Security, and investments.* Think again. Ten checks in retirement is better than the three-legged stool.

10. *Bonds are safe.* Only government-backed bonds are guaranteed but you may not make much.

11. *Dollar cost averaging is the way to amass wealth.* If you are not careful, dollar cost averaging may end up being dollar-lost averaging.

12. *Diversify according to Modern Portfolio Theory's pie among 60 percent stock and 40 percent bond.* The pie is a lie. It failed in 2008 and may fail again. Consider diversification trading strategies, not just assets.

13. *The only things certain in life are death and taxes.* You can leave money that is income- and death tax–free.

14. *Take only 4 percent a year out of your savings after you retire.* The good old 4 percent rule. Forget it. We'll see why in chapter 13.

15. *Disability will never happen to me and long-term-care insurance is just too costly.* Disability and long-term-care insurance makes sure you don't spend all of your wealth on your health in your later years.

16. *All you need is a will, and you are okay if you die.* Estate planning is the ultimate act of planning for the people and causes you love.

The following are two lists contrasting the old reality with the new retirement reality check:

REALITY CHECK

If what you thought to be true about money turned out not to be so, when would you want to know?

OLD REALITY

1   Skip the lattes and the vacation.

2   Taxes are inescapable; max out your 401(k) to a qualified retirement plan.

3   Buy term insurance and invest the difference between whole life and term premiums.

4   Avoid annuities—"I'd rather die and go to hell than buy an annuity."

5   Monte Carlo Simulation is all you need.

6   Set up a budget.

7   Drawdowns are a part of life.

8   I will rely on the three-legged-stool of pension, Social Security, and investments.

9   Bonds are safe enough.

10 Dollar cost averaging is a pillar of investing.

11 Diversification/60–40, the pie is proven.

12 You can't escape taxes when you die.

13 Four percent is the proper amount to withdraw from your accounts when you retire.

14 Disability will never happen to me and long-term-care insurance is just too costly.

15 I don't want to think about death planning, but I'll just get a will when I get around to it.

NEW REALITY

1 Enjoy today and tomorrow.

2 Mitigate taxes wherever possible. Max out your retirement plan, but only after you've protected your family. Until then, contribute to your retirement up to the company match, then plow the rest of your savings into tax-smart Roths and cash-value life insurance.

3 Cash-value life insurance is a secret of the rich. Some call it the "Rich Person's Roth." Buy term life for protection of your family (20 times your salary) and cash-value life insurance for tax-smart accumulation. Consider a mutual insurer that pays dividends. Then, invest the rest.

4 Annuities can be the pension you never had but always wanted. They make sure you never outlive your money. New and improved annuities have low costs, too, and leave money to your heirs when you die.

5 Process always precedes products. Spend more in the early years of retirement when you have your health and your wealth and can enjoy life. The right annuities coupled with the spend-down strategy allows you to enjoy your money in the here and now. Go to Italy!

6 Set up autosave accounts for giving, saving, and living.

7 Set up a volatility buffer so that when bad times come you can pull money from it.

8 Set up a 10-check retirement plan.

9 Bonds come with certain risks.

10 Beware of dollar-lost averaging.

11 The pie is a lie. In the last downturn, stocks and bonds both went down. Diversify not just assets but strategies.

12 Spend-down strategies help you spend more than the 4 percent rule.

13 Annuities may give you more money to spend on the things you enjoy in retirement.

14 Disability and long-term-care insurance makes sure you don't spend all of your wealth on your health.

15 Estate planning is the ultimate act of planning for the people you love and the causes you love.

REALITY CHECK

When you focus on retirement, the old rules don't apply anymore. You need a retirement reality check, and that is exactly the book that we will give you. Here are the new realities we're going to talk about:

1. Quit worrying about your money. Most retirement planning advice is wrong.
2. Mitigate the onslaught of income taxes with our 11-step approach.
3. Buy term life insurance and invest the difference vs. buy whole and invest the rest.
4. Annuities aren't the devil: they can deliver 30 percent more income in retirement. Annuities are your friend.
5. Monte Carlo is for gambling, not wise money management. An easy-to-understand game plan will organize your finances.
6. Start saving and don't let fear drive your investing train!
7. Don't lose money in the next stock market crash. Create a volatility buffer.
8. How to generate 10 checks in retirement by creating new revenue streams.
9. Bonds may be a recipe for disaster. Get out of bond jail. Take AIM (see page 14).
10. Forget dollar cost averaging.
11. Diversification could lead to di-worsification.
12. Retire in the ZERO tax bracket. A well-thought-out spend-down strategy will get you there.
13. Conservative withdrawal strategies can generate 30 percent more income for retirement. Forget the 4 percent rule.

14.   Protect your money from disability and the nursing home.

15.   Estate planning: What is that?

But wait, Josh, you might be thinking now. *Why should I leave the conventional rules to follow yours?*

This book is meant to be a game plan. These are discussion points for you and your spouse, significant other, or advisor. These are topics to think about and bring up rather than "it says on page 87 that I have to do exactly *x*, *y*, and *z*," because everybody's circumstances are different and financial circumstances and laws change all the time.

At the end of chapter 2, you'll do a self-assessment that will change your approach to your finances and enable you to retire the way you want to.

WE ALL NEED A PLAN

Begin with the end in mind. Everyone needs to plan for retirement, whether millennial or boomer. If you're just starting out, living from paycheck to paycheck, still trying to pay off student loans, and have no clue how you'll ever have enough saved to stop working, you'll find sensible and understandable ideas on how best to put your money away. If you've managed to save some money, you'll find out how to put it to work. If you're getting ready to retire but not sure that $100,000 or $500,000 or $1 million will be enough, you'll find dozens of ideas on how to minimize taxes legally and build your savings so you can spend as you wish.

The best retirement plans are *designed*, not just cobbled together, and *design takes strategic thinking*. Just buying a magic product won't assure your financial happiness. The process may be a little time-consuming, but any real retirement solution requires a deliberate and well-thought-out mix of investments that may include bonds, exchange-traded funds, mutual funds, stocks, insurance policies, and real estate; and a variety of strategies, which will change with circumstances, to minimize taxes over time. It all needs to work together. You need The Financial Quarterback™ to help put it together.

What if I told you we could get you *30 percent more income than your current portfolio*? Think about it—30 percent greater income! What if I showed you a way to get yourself in a tax-efficient position where you would pay zero taxes in retirement? What if I could show you 10 different ways to save on your taxes legally? What if I could show you a way to get massive deductions on your tax return? What if I could show you a way to get three times the interest you get on CDs at the bank?

Now, that ought to whet your appetite!

YOUR FINANCIAL BLUEPRINT: SWING VS. CLUBS

If you want a blueprint for financial success written for an everyday layperson, this book is for you. You won't find a phony get-rich-quick scheme, but practical advice for a more conservative financial future.

If you had the choice, would you rather get trained by a legendary golf pro like Tiger Woods to take three strokes off your score, or would you rather own the best set of golf clubs? In this book, although we educate you on financial products (the clubs) to own, we're focusing on the swing of protection, tax minimization, and income planning. Enhanced swings will give you a better game regardless of what clubs you use. You need the swing, not the clubs.

This is the one book that you could leave to your spouse or significant other and say, "Hey, you know what? If anything happens to me, do what this book says, and you will have a financial game plan."

I'm going to show you:

- how to get up to 10 checks in retirement that you aren't getting now.
- ways to mitigate risk so that if we have another market crash, you don't lose your principal.
- how to create a pool of cash, called a volatility buffer, no matter how old you are and how much money you have to start.

We'll use tools including annuities, insurance (life insurance), and managed investments—think of the acronym AIM—to store this money away, so that you have a buffer of financial security no matter what happens in the stock market.

Then we'll look at 10 new ways for anyone to generate more cash from the cash they already have, give you 11 ways to legally minimize taxes on your retirement stash (most of which require some planning ahead), and show you how to set up a spend-down strategy that will give you more money to spend each year, while still allowing for growth.

These strategies all but blow up conventional financial planning wisdom. If you listen to these people, you're supposed to scrimp, save, and essentially make yourself unhappy in order to pay off credit-card and student debt. When you retire, you're supposed to spend 4 percent a year, not 10 percent, and you won't get that 4 percent back. Annuities are too expensive and risky. Life insurance is only good if you die—you pay all those premiums—and you only benefit when you're dead! Just put most of your money in index funds and bonds and forget it.

SAYS WHO?

Who am I to tell you that the conventional advice has been misguided, and I know better?

I'm a guy who started out with $60,000 in credit-card debt, became a millionaire in my twenties by saving a large portion of my income and road-testing many of the strategies I recommend, and spent the last two decades helping my clients turn around their finances and their lives. I now have a volatility buffer, multiple income streams, a safe spend-down strategy for my eventual retirement, ample amounts of the right kind of insurance, and solid tax, health-care, and estate planning strategies. You can do this, too.

I dispense advice one-on-one and over the radio and on television appearances. Since I've never found my holistic approach in another book, I decided to write this one.

BACK TO KENNY

Let's revisit Kenny to explore one way this all works.

He and I met at the Lobster Shanty in Toms River, New Jersey, at a financial planning seminar I hosted to educate people at or nearing retirement. We immediately hit it off. Kenny was squeamish—to say the least—and wary of getting near another guy like me. He told me he had attended the seminar to absorb as much information as he could, since he wanted to start managing his own retirement account because of his bad experiences.

Kenny, a big, burly guy in a plaid flannel shirt and dungarees, worked for the Budweiser plant that everybody sees when they fly into the Newark Airport in New Jersey. He was a single dad, raising three children. He lost his wife at a young age but maintained a sense of pride in being there for his children. Kenny worked hard to support his family. He even worked two shifts at the Budweiser brewery to cover day care and later picked up another job to send them to college.

Kenny thoughtfully and carefully saved and built a nest egg of nearly a million dollars. He loved to save all his change in big jars, and a few times a year, he would bring dozens of rolls of quarters, dimes, nickels, and pennies to the bank to turn into paper money and deposit in his account. The tellers would spot him as soon as he lumbered into the bank with his rolls of coins and get ready for the long count.

He trusted his fortune to an advisor at his bank, blindly letting this person manage his retirement savings. Kenny lost almost half of his portfolio during the market correction of 2002, because his advisor kept him heavy in the stock market.

He responded the same way many people do who lose money in a stock downturn. He sold stock, shifting almost all his money to a more conservative strategy with a lower interest, relying a lot on certificates of deposit. He did that, and sure enough, we watched the market go up, up, and away, gaining about 40 percent from 2003 to 2006, while he was locked into his 3 percent a year. He felt like he was losing out, and so did his advisor.

They again decided to market-time and swing the other way, putting most of his money back into the market. Everything was booming, and Kenny wanted to enjoy the same recovery as his friends. You can guess the rest of the story. Just as he regained trust in the stock market and bought in, the market crashed again and for the second time Kenny lost half of his portfolio.

Once again, Kenny was a victim of bad timing and reactionary investing.

Kenny hadn't done anything wrong. The financial planning industry in this country has been broken for a long time, and he just fell victim to it. For the past 30 years or so, people have been taught to react to the latest trend, diversify their money according to a 60-year-old theory, deny themselves small pleasures like lattes in order to slowly and painfully pay down credit-card debt, and generally drain all joy out of working, saving, and living.

Everything normal people like to do—such as taking a vacation or treating the family to dinner or replacing that gasping old jalopy—was to be denied in order to gradually chip away at credit-card debt. If you ever managed to pay it off, you were supposed to put your savings into index funds or bonds yielding no more than 3 percent. You needed to limit your retirement spending to 4 percent of your principal a year, no matter what. If you didn't fulfill your dreams doing that, tough.

And if that wasn't impractical enough, some of these gurus promised to not just get you out of debt, but also to make you rich. Most conventional financial planning focuses on the financial product that will make you rich.

A JOYLESS DIET

What an unrelenting diet of joyless and soul-destroying advice!

Through all this, I started to see that the finance planning paradigm was off a bit. Thirty or 40 years after the dawn of the financial self-help industry, the average person I run into every day is no better off.

People have been following the same recycled ideas from the financial celebrities you may hear on radio or see on TV. If we look at the landscape of financial planning in America, the crisis has never been greater. These books teach you to diversify, buy and hold, die broke when you're old, don't enjoy today, and leave all your money to your kids, even when your kids may not have the best relationship with you. They don't speak to the nonconventional financial plan or nontraditional family. They tell you that you need to have a million dollars, and only spend 4 percent of it a year when you retire.

But what if you could live off both principal and interest and still leave all your principal to your kids or your favorite charity? How would you like to live on 30 percent more income with the same assets?

This book will show you how to do this.

Maybe you'll never attain the mythical retirement you dream of. But you should enjoy your days on this earth. You should have memories with your kids and grandkids. Maybe you don't have to retire at 62. Maybe you want to take a vacation every year in your 30s and 40s and retire at 70.

The point of this book is to give you options.

The tools we'll discuss—ETFs, stocks, bonds, annuities, whole life insurance, whatever—are really just places to store money to offset the effects of inflation and wealth-eroding factors, such as a stock market decline, personal disability, early death of you or your spouse, and something nobody thinks about until it's too late, planned obsolescence risk—your refrigerator is definitely going to break before you expect it to.

You're not going to get rich protecting yourself from all these risks, but that's the heart of financial planning and it's going to let you sleep a lot better.

I got out of debt in six months and haven't looked back. My wife and I tried to be frugal, but we never scrimped. We went out to dinner once a week—hello, Outback!—and we took a once-a-year "honeymoon" trip to a nice resort, often in the Caribbean or Mexico. We ate healthy food—usually chicken or salmon bought on sale at the Acme, cooked on a George Foreman Grill—but never had to live on instant ramen noodles.

We'll show you how to establish what I call a fulcrum of protection. You may remember from physics class that a fulcrum is what the lever rests on and gives it the power to move a great weight. For financial planning, that fulcrum comes from having a nest egg—I call it a volatility buffer—which may include the right kinds of insurance and conservative investments. It doesn't have to be huge, but it has great power.

This book is based on the economic principle of certainty. If you have the proper amounts of certainty in your life, you can end up taking greater risks because you are hedged. If you were to become disabled, you would still be okay. If you lead with a bias toward protection, you can have the freedom to invest in your life, maybe even become an entrepreneur. If you just took care of your worries with 30 percent to 40 percent of your nest egg, you would have the freedom to invest the rest in your future. You want disability insurance equal to two-thirds of your current income—that way it will equate to your after-tax earning power. If you do not have the principle of economic certainty in your life, then "Do not pass Go. Do not collect $200." It was only after I secured a disability insurance and life insurance policy that I had the confidence to hurl myself into my business—accumulating and then paying off $60,000 in credit-card debt—without worrying about uncertainty.

Do this and you'll never have to take much risk to live serenely.

When I started making money, that fulcrum of protection let me be a bit more aggressive in my 401(k) investments, to take more chances with my business, to take entrepreneurial risk. You could do the same.

If you don't have to worry so much about the future, you can take advantage of more opportunity in the present. And you may even sleep better.

MEET ED AND NANCY

Ed and Nancy are a charming Long Island couple, now in their 60s, the salt of the earth. They go to Catholic Mass every Sunday and live by the Good Book. They're good, patriotic Americans. They'll write you a Christmas card every year. If they were your neighbors, they would show up at your aunt's funeral. They'll send you a Catholic Mass card when you're going through a hard time. They're genuinely nice people.

And when they came to see me, I could see the anguish in Nancy's eyes. Ed thought he didn't have enough money to retire, and all she wanted was to be able to spend a good 10 or 15 years with her husband.

They had about $2 million and a paid-off house, but Ed kept applying the darned 4 percent rule in his head. "Okay, if I have two million at 4 percent, I'm only gonna make 80 grand a year for the rest of my life, plus Social Security." That's about $120,000. He knows he needs $150,000 to live the way he wants.

We showed him how to get $150,000 from the same assets instead of $120,000. Now he can retire in three years. Even more than retiring in three years, he has a new set of spectacles with which to look at the world.

They recently came back from a trip to Italy and he called me. "Josh, you changed my life. I went to Italy. I didn't look at my phone. I truly was present for 12 days with my family; it was the best 12 days of my life."

Ed, like many others, had been stuck in the failed ways of financial planning.

The biggest problem with many popular plans is that they're not *holistic*. Holistic plans consider all aspects of a problem. Popular plans, in contrast, don't view your whole life as a continuum of 80 short years on this earth. They want you to defer enjoyment, but for what? Lots of people won't even start on a financial plan because they think they must deprive themselves forever.

You can't just focus on the growth of the money; you should focus on the *enjoyment* of the money. It's not how to accumulate money, but rather how to distribute the money.

As you'll see later, I can show you how to spend 30 percent more money in your retirement and leave the same amount of money you would have left under the old paradigm.

In all I do, I always involve my clients, from the initial interviews to every step of the planning process to changing course when necessary for whatever reason. This book will be no different.

If you're as nervous and fretful as Kenny was, then read on and hear the rest of Kenny's story.

A FAMILIAR STORY

Kenny was far from alone in suffering health problems from a financial setback. A study by Northwestern University's medical school in Chicago found that middle-aged folks who suffered a big financial loss were more than 50 percent more likely to die in the few years following the shock than people who didn't suffer a downturn in their financial fortunes.[1] Financial stress can lead to heart disease and strokes, among other bad stuff.

Kenny's story struck a chord with me, since it was an all-too-familiar one. Like many of his baby-boomer colleagues, Kenny was the victim of flawed planning, a poor strategy, and a nearsighted approach. But after talking for a few minutes during one of the seminar breaks, we agreed to schedule a meeting for later that week. Kenny made it clear that he wasn't committing to work with me, but he was willing to at least listen to what I had to say. I certainly couldn't blame him, since Kenny couldn't even stand the mention of the words "financial" and "advisor."

He eventually provided me with his home address, and I agreed to drive off the beaten path to a small town in Pennsylvania, right outside of New Jersey, to meet him. As I matched the address on the mailbox to the one I had scribbled down on a small legal pad, I pulled into the concrete driveway and parked my car in front of his modest and well-kept home. I knocked on his front door, and Kenny greeted me with what could only be described as a look of resignation.

He still could barely stand the thought of me. We exchanged handshakes, and he invited me in. I found myself sitting on an oversized couch in a modestly furnished family room with a gas fireplace and a wet bar. I sat directly across from Kenny, and it felt like I was taking his daughter to the prom and about to get the "speech." But shortly after getting comfortable, Kenny leaned back and started to pepper me with questions.

"How long ya been doing this?" A good question, since I was then only 27.

"What are your fees?" I explained the structure.

"Can I lose my money again?" Yes, but we'll work together to make sure this is unlikely.

I answered question after question, half of which aimed at defending financial advisors as a whole. It wasn't an easy exchange, but I did my best to provide answers in an open and honest manner. I shared my background with Kenny and explained my theory of retirement investing, which you'll find in this book.

It didn't take long for him to warm up to me, and we even shared a few laughs about some of the endless struggles Kenny had had with his previous advisors. It had all played out like a Shakespearean tragedy—blood everywhere.

Or maybe a *Die Hard* movie: "If ya lose this money, I'll kill you," he joked. At least, I hoped he was joking.

THE KEY THING

As Kenny opened up to me, the more I realized that we totally understood each other. What he most wanted was a SWAN (sleep well at night) account while getting a decent but conservative return on all those quarters he had so lovingly rolled and turned in to the bank. I could do that and recommended a conservative approach that might help restore his trust in financial advisors.

It was obvious that what he was doing—everything was in cash—wasn't going to get him enough income or financial security to lead to the retirement he longed for. Kenny, a widower with grown kids, had two goals: to be able to travel in Europe (his family, like the original Budweiser, was Czech and had ties to a picturesque village in what had been Bohemia, which he'd never seen) and to restore more old cars like the 1952 Plymouth sedan I saw peeking out of his garage.

Kenny was the victim of a bad spend-down strategy and not maintaining a volatility buffer. (We'll talk a lot more about both these things later in the book.) We spent almost two hours together that evening. We spoke about the missteps and mistakes his advisors had made on his behalf. The Coke was cold, the gas fire was warm, and we started to bond.

It took a total of 14 meetings over many months—I told you Kenny distrusted financial advisors!—but Kenny eventually trusted me to help him live without the fear of losing it all.

My team went right to work. We rebalanced his portfolio, which was $1 million, all in cash, created a volatility buffer that we agreed to fund each month, and segmented his investments.

THIS IS NOW . . .

That was 10 years ago. Today, Kenny is living off his nest egg, has been to his Czech homeland, and has added a '63 Corvette and a '65 Mustang to his Plymouth. He has almost no money in the stock market—just conservative investments throwing off cash. Although that strategy might not be right for everyone, Kenny is gaining back years of his life. He doesn't have to watch CNBC every day, a go-to habit for millions of viewers worried about their money. The cold sweats and night tremors are gone. Kenny is coasting and resting easy.

He's been a happy client to this day. He's satisfied with his average 4 percent return because he's got all kinds of protection and buffers that let him enjoy life and live without fear. He doesn't have to worry about the market plunging anymore. Yes, he may have missed out on the most recent market rally, but the 4 percent is good by him. He's comfortable, and that is what matters. Kenny is now able to enjoy his money for the first time in his life. Kenny's story paints a common picture—no single strategy works for every person every time. Investors and their various needs are just as unique and different as the variety of investment options out there.

Throughout this book, you'll read about a lot of people like Kenny, and while none of them may mirror your situation exactly, the strategies and insights you'll find will give you ideas for your own strategies, and prompt lots of questions to ask your own advisors, just as Kenny asked me that night in his family room and in 13 more sessions before he hired me.

MEET DONALD AND SHERYL

Donald and Sheryl were the classiest, most debonair, most devoted Christian couple I'd ever encountered. I never saw Donald when he wasn't dressed impeccably, like the old-school New York City salesman that he'd been for 50 years. From a famous store, he outfitted Wall Street bankers for half a century.

They came to me a couple of years before Donald's retirement. They had a couple hundred thousand dollars made from flipping houses back when that real estate strategy was profitable. Sheryl wanted most to travel, something they had rarely managed to do while Donald was working. She wanted to go to Greece, her ancestral homeland, and to Alaska.

Sadly, Donald died from leukemia that was misdiagnosed. They never got to travel to Greece or Alaska. I still remember what Sheryl said to me at his viewing. It was one of the most tragic things I've ever heard a woman say: "I wish we could have gone to Greece together." To her, it wasn't just a vacation but a culmination of years spent sacrificing for their kids. This was supposed to be their time. The expression on her face was etched into my soul. Plan so that you can enjoy tomorrow and today.

While nothing could bring Donald back, we designed a strategy for Sheryl, not unlike what we had for Kenny, that would let her live money-worry free for the rest of her life. It may have been a small comfort, but it was a comfort.

Plan early. Every day is precious. Enjoy your money while you can.

ENJOY YOUR MONEY

The big idea—hammered into my head by my dealings with Kenny and Donald and Sheryl and Ed and Nancy and the thousands of people I've met in the last 15 years or so—is this: the majority of people with $500,000 to $1 million to their name just don't want to worry.

They'll accept, maybe grudgingly, a lower rate of return than they see others getting, so long as their money grows conservatively and is enough for them to live a happy and fulfilled life.

Many people just don't think they have enough money, no matter what amount they have. They may have that $500,000 to $1 million but are afraid to invest it in case they'll lose it, and afraid to spend it because they know it will be gone. But with a sound savings and spend-down strategy involving Social Security, income streams, the proper amounts of protection, and sound investments, many of you can enjoy a healthy income stream that will empower you to do what you enjoy. It just takes thought and planning.

Too many people don't think much about retirement before they retire. People in their 20s and 30s don't have the money, nor do they have a sense of what they really enjoy doing. People in their 40s and 50s know what they enjoy but may not have enough money yet. So they wait until they are 65 or 70 to retire. It makes some sense: by this age they have some wealth and they know what's important to them. But it leaves them maybe only 10 to 15 years to enjoy the fruits of all those years of work.

It's vital to consider life expectancy in retirement planning, which nobody ever does. The average life expectancy is currently about 78 years for a man and 82 years for a woman. If you're a guy who retires at 65, you've got about a decade left. (Sure, people live to 100 or more—God bless them—but these wonders are relatively rare.)

The key to a happy retirement is having the resources and security to find and do what you love. It's not just having the most toys. It might involve still working, but most often it will involve a hobby or a charity or a cause that has been important to you, that you didn't have time for while building a career. I've run into people dedicated to causes as varied as the local shul and the Chicago Cubs. Some retirees want to travel, and others want to make sure they'll never lose their paid-off home in order to move into a nursing home. Others want to stay home and know they will be able to care for each other.

This book will show you how to retire and enjoy your money for 20 to 30 years. It takes the correct financial products and a sound spend-down strategy, a term we'll return to often.

It's divided into four parts: Start Your Retirement Reality Check, Save It!, Spend 'Til the End, and Leave It!

In turn, the "Start Your Retirement Reality Check" part is divided into stand-alone chapters on an 11-step approach to mitigating taxes, a new way to look at insuring your assets, annuities as a way to create a pension for yourself, developing The Ultimate Financial Game Plan for yourself, and how to save and get out of debt.

The "Save It!" part focuses on creating and maintaining a volatility buffer; developing new revenue streams; and shaking off the outdated notions that everyone should buy and hold index funds or low-yielding bonds and pour good money after bad in a sour market, hoping to dollar-cost-average your way out of a problem.

The "Spend 'Til the End" part will explain and give many examples of conservative spend-down strategies, which take advantage of all legal and tax-efficient ways to start spending the money you've saved as you actually stop worrying and start enjoying your retirement. It's everybody's goal, but a shockingly small number of people do it correctly. This section will also explain why the famous 4 percent rule—that you should spend down only 4 percent of your capital each year—deserves to be sent to the same graveyard as rotary-dial phones and telex machines.

The "Leave It!" section will look at the two vital areas of planning that everyone needs to take care of well before they retire. These areas apply to anyone, whether they want to leave all their fortune to the grandkids or the Metropolitan Museum or let the last check bounce after the hearse drops you off at the cemetery. Healthcare planning can make all the difference between a comfortable and a miserable retirement. Estate planning in many cases can let you have your cake and eat it, too, by letting you do everything you want to do in retirement and still have something to pass on.

2008 REDUX?

This book is being written a decade after the worst financial recession most of us have ever experienced. With each passing year, we gain valuable insight into years past. The financial crisis in 2008 was a learning opportunity. We might not be able to avoid a terrible downturn in the market again, but we can learn from investors past to ensure we respond in a more strategic manner.

So many financial advisors manage the money of their clients using old strategies in ways that don't account for the human element and ignore the financial goals of their clients. Everyone subscribing to the same investment strategies all of the time would be like a doctor treating every patient with the same medicine, regardless of the disease. Generally speaking, the concepts of investing, saving, and retirement haven't changed, *but the way we hedge against risk has.* We now have many new financial tools.

TEND YOUR GARDEN

A retirement portfolio is like a garden in that it will eventually wither away if you do not tend to it. A financial advisor can't just plant the seeds and walk away, expecting to see a bed of flowers a few months later.

Many of the once-accepted rules are the result of poor planning and lazy financial planners. They serve the planner well because they make money regardless of performance. The inevitable and unavoidable victim is the retiree. These guys and gals managing your money don't have a bad motive—they are just comfortable and some may be reliant on bad information.

I subscribe to a different philosophy. I am here to buck the trend and say: "Wait a second . . . this doesn't work. Take a step back and consider whether this investing strategy is really the one you want to bet on."

I started my business many years ago. However, my experience wasn't colored by the growth of the eighties and tech-boom nineties.

Rather, it took a giant kick in the face—2001 and then 2008. Those are my early memories of planning. I saw the blood in the streets. I watched two market crashes turn into a lost decade for equities and decimate nest eggs—years and years of smart saving only to be washed away by one giant financial reset. Most recently, I am seeing new innovations in asset allocation and income planning. These are fresh and exciting ideas aimed at progress to evolve our fundamental investment practices, and I'm going to share them with you. Yet too often we continue to rely on conventional concepts that may set us up for failure.

EMPOWER YOUR PORTFOLIO

This book carries the purpose of helping you empower your portfolio with better savings strategies and well-conceptualized withdrawal approaches. I am not preaching miracles. Rather, we aim to secure a better understanding of options and opportunity. This is your nest egg, and it is time to rise up and do everything you can to protect it.

Throughout this book, we'll visit a bunch of everyday examples. You may see yourself in their shoes. Kenny might decide that a conservative rate of return with lower volatility is the right fit for him. Brenda might take on greater risk for greater potential returns because she's got a number of different volatility buffers—safe savings vehicles—in place. Alan and Ashley had a strategy; it just couldn't stand up against the 2008 debacle. Jeffrey and Maureen just wanted to take care of each other. Patti didn't trust any advisor. Successful investors are clear on their needs, and fantastic advisors listen and respond. They don't blindly subscribe to the herd mentality—like the 4 percent rule—because it isn't right for everyone.

The smartest investors and advisors begin with the end in mind. The very smartest ones aim to enjoy their money and their life both before and after retirement. This book is for you.

START NOW

Retirement planning shouldn't start at retirement age, or even in your 40s. It should start now. It's never too late or too early.

A shocking number of Americans have absolutely no retirement savings at age 60. A recent report said that the median (the same number of people below the number and above it) retirement savings of Americans between the ages of 56 and 61 is $25,000!

The average (there are people with zero and people with a whole lot) for the 44-to-49-year-old age group is around $81,000. That's better, but it's not much better. And I'm increasingly seeing millennials (those born between about 1980 and 2005) who have saved some serious money but have had it all in cash—missing out on the 2000–2007 and 2009–2018 stock market booms.

There are also some millennials who haven't managed to save anything. According to figures from the St. Louis Fed, the cohort born in the 1980s had wealth more than 30 percent below what their predecessor generations had at the same age. Blame slow wage growth, rising rents, and student loans. The same will likely be true of the next generation.

Even in a steady to accelerating economy since 2009, paychecks haven't grown much beyond inflation, and hardly anybody can afford to sock much away. The Fed's Report on the Economic Well-Being of US Households in 2017 showed that a quarter of people had no retirement savings at all, and that 40 percent of households couldn't scrape together $400 in cash to meet an emergency. (It was even worse in 2013, when 50 percent said they couldn't do this.)

And this mass of people may not be able to depend as much on what the boomers could—Social Security and Medicare. Within 15 years or so, Social Security payments will need to be trimmed, absent action from Congress. Medicare faces similar pressure.

WHAT TO DO?

Retirement saving should begin in your 20s and 30s. You grow your volatility buffer early in your career so you have it available to you if you need to spend it for college, or disability, or an unexpected issue. You should start segmenting, or diversifying, your investments long before you actually retire, to hedge against risk. You should diversify from day one so you can protect your savings from the tidal waves of financial destruction. And finally, you don't blindly pledge to follow one theory 100 percent of the time, even if your financial advisor promises you it is foolproof and time-tested.

Any strategy that doesn't account for market correction and significant downturn should be buried in the financial graveyard. The first mistake most investors make is not planning for volatility. We often refer to that as a volatility buffer, and each and every investor should have one built into his or her retirement strategy.

If you're saving for the whole purpose of living off your pot of gold, you're not saving to simply give it all back because you just couldn't see the writing on the wall. Question your advisor to better understand your spend-down strategy (if you even have a spend-down strategy). Ask about your volatility buffer and determine if you are protecting against the turbulent times ahead. If your advisor tells you not to worry, ask again for specifics. Remember Kenny and those 14 meetings? Ask and ask again until you understand. Otherwise your plans may fail. It is not a question of if; it is a matter of how soon.

As you'll see throughout the book, there are steps you can take during the course of your savings and moving into retirement that can help you alleviate risk and sleep soundly. There are millions of people looking for a conservative alternative to bonds or cash and want to get off the risk elevator.

To disregard this would be equivalent to playing Russian roulette with your retirement. Yet people do it each day of their lives without explanation. They blindly follow their veteran advisor into retirement hell, even when there were signs and flashing lights along the way indicating that they should turn around and go back.

Let's preview a couple of strategies to ensure you don't fall victim to a tsunami of financial disparity. We'll address these in detail later.

THE VOLATILITY BUFFER

It is important to create certain safeguards to supplement your drawdown retirement policy. It could be cash, it could be treasuries, it could be a fixed annuity, or it could be something like cash value from a life insurance policy. A volatility buffer is something you can draw down for either something you need (like responding to a financial crisis) or for something you want (like a cruise to Alaska). This can be especially helpful in the first few years of retirement, where a tsunami could cause the most damage to your retirement savings. Losses earlier in retirement can be more devastating than losses later in retirement. Don't just wait until your retirement to create a volatility buffer. By then, it may be too late.

For example, if you intend to draw money from a life insurance policy during a financial crisis, that policy will be much less expensive the younger you are. If you planned accordingly and bought the policy in your 30s, you'll have a less expensive and better-funded policy in place when you retire. If you prefer having a straight cash buffer, start setting aside money today in cash with an ultimate goal of one to two years of living expenses in that buffer. Find a high-yield money market fund (shop rates on bankrate.com) and sock away a thousand dollars per month. You may have over $400,000 in free cash when you retire. You can decide to use some of that cash to pay your bills, fund other investments, or just spend on non-incidentals like vacation or gifts to your family. Think about how safe you might feel with this supplementing your retirement savings as a separate "break in case of emergency" mechanism.

RISK POOLING

This is a way to diversify. For example, you might decide to put 60 percent of your portfolio in fixed income investments like annuities, investment-grade bonds, or life insurance, while leaving the other 40 percent in higher-growth-potential exchange-traded funds or no-load mutual funds. It might also make sense for you to split your investment portfolio among different investments with varying management strategies. The point in risk pooling is to spread your exposure around investments that react differently to market forces, so that one catastrophic correction doesn't wipe out your entire retirement account. Financial geeks call this noncorrelation. As John Mauldin puts it, "proper risk management is about diversifying not just asset classes but also trading strategies."

Each of these shifts in your retirement planning should not just help you save, but also protect your hard-earned nest egg. That is the ultimate lesson of this book: earn but protect. Those tsunamis are coming, and we should all make considerate and thoughtful investments to ensure that we are prepared when they come crashing down on our portfolios. As Stephen King says, "There's no harm in hoping for the best as long as you're prepared for the worst."

Failure isn't fun. For most, it is a horrifying reality with which they eventually come to terms in some capacity in their lives. No one can completely avoid failure, but we should do all we can to minimize it. When it comes to investing and retirement, failure can come in many shapes and sizes. It can be the investor who didn't save enough over the course of his or her professional career and cannot afford to retire. Or there is the investor who saved some, but not enough to support the same quality of life they lived while still working. And maybe the most difficult form of failure to swallow—when an investor does everything right, only to watch his or her retirement get washed away by one big and unexpected financial meltdown.

THE STENCH OF FAILURE

The goal of this book is to remove the stench of failure and renew your faith in setting goals and using the right tools and strategies to get you there. We'll show you how to raise, keep, and—most importantly—spend money on the things that make you happy and make the whole notion of retirement worthwhile. Your retirement should be built over the years, with careful placement and consideration. It should give you joy, not heartburn.

Failing to protect against the big waves is almost certainly a recipe for disaster. In all this, the most challenging pill to choke down is that you could have avoided the wave altogether if you had made better decisions along the way. Failure comes in all different shapes and sizes, but you don't have to be a victim to flawed investment strategies. You can be part of the smaller, yet empowered, group of investors that bucked the trends, saw the light, and realized that old tools can often be outdated ones.

Life insurance is morbid and boring. Bonds are even more boring than insurance and might be something your grandparents owned. Annuities tie up your money and don't earn that much. A volatility buffer sounds like something you'd have to jump over in a video game.

Too many times, people don't model out their financial game plan. They create a pie chart or use a calculator on a website, and they consider that financial planning. It's not a holistic model based on the theory that whatever can go wrong probably will and that life is uncertain. You have to model out numerous scenarios and test your plan to make sure it holds up under a variety of circumstances.

WHAT DOES MONEY MEAN TO YOU?

The key to solving financial problems is for you to assess your situation honestly and reflect on experiences in your life that have shaped your view of money. What has made you particularly stingy or maybe a spendthrift?

Imagine living your life based on the thought that your dad could die at any time. Over nearly 30 years of my own life, indeed my entire financial future, has been shaped by the impending demise of my father, who suffered a heart attack when I was only 11. You might consider that a depressing thought—and understandably so. Allow me to explain. Although I deeply miss my mom and dad, they shaped my reality. My father encouraged me to be a man of faith by his example in word and deed. Knowing about his impending death became liberating because I began with the end in mind. This perspective instilled in me a lifelong view of money as protection, against illness specifically, but also against unhappiness in general. It's not the money itself; it's the security and peace of mind it can buy.

My view of money has been shaped by my faith that money is not the end of life, but a tool to bless the people and the causes you love.

So as my faith and parents shaped my financial life, I am drawn to strategies that protect my wife and kids and provide for them in times of emergency. Because I saw my father go through some unfortunate events without a volatility buffer, without a personal pension, and with term insurance that expired before he passed, I dedicated my life to learning and educating clients on protection programs. Conventional planning wisdom did nothing to protect him from the big three risks—disability, unemployment, and death. I want to set you up with a plan that works whether you become disabled or unemployed, or you die. When you cover the big three, you can live for today. You can enjoy the present because the uncertain tomorrow is taken care of.

Your trigger motivation may be completely different, but I hope this book convinces you that breaking old habits and creating and following a strategy that can lower risk and let you sleep at night, knowing that your most important concerns have been taken care of, is a good thing.

The possibilities we'll see are a steady flow of income when you need it, protection against wealth-eroding risks, and the satisfaction of leaving a legacy.

The means to achieve these possibilities are detailed in the rest of this book. These include considering the right kind of steady, income-oriented savings that will create a volatility buffer to protect against emergencies; new revenue streams coming from investments or cash that you already have; and new ways of thinking about such investment strategies as putting all your money in fixed-income investments like bonds, spending only 4 percent of your income a year after you retire, and throwing good money after bad when your stocks go down. They also include developing conservative spend-down strategies that may yield you a lot more than 4 percent a year, and how to ensure that you leave money how and where you want to through sound tax, health, and estate planning.

ACTION STEPS

- Use the examples in this book to develop a holistic retirement strategy.
- Take the investment profile quiz, which shows how you should allocate your investments given your objectives, at retirementrealitycheck.com.
- It is not enough to save or spend wisely. You also must factor in the drawdown risk in any investment.
- Hold your financial advisor accountable by regularly asking questions and learning about saving/retirement strategies.
- Hedge against risk early in your saving career, using strategies like a volatility buffer, segmentation, and portfolio diversification.
- Ask yourself this question: Would you rather incorporate a plan that prevents you from ever being poor, or a plan designed to make you rich, but you could lose your shirt? In other words, are you more motivated by security or risk/opportunity?
- Would you rather have a sure thing or a maybe (as retirement specialist Mike Steranka puts it)?
- A financial reset may be coming in our economic system—are you prepared?

REALITY CHECK

MITIGATE THE ONSLAUGHT OF INCOME TAXES WITH OUR 11-STEP APPROACH.

MEET RAY AND HELEN

Ray and Helen are a couple in their 30s who started and ran a lucrative chain of home-furnishing stores in the Philadelphia area. Their typical profit after all expenses was $500,000 a year, all taxable.

Small-business owners often take a beating from the Internal Revenue Service (IRS), and Ray and Helen were no exception.

Their accountant had advised them to start a 401(k), but that was only going to give them a $19,000 write-off.

We advised them a bit differently.

We developed a strategy both for now and for when they retire in 30 years or so. You've got to think about both.

First, we created a cash-balance pension plan, which under the 2006 Pension Protection Act allows small-business owners in their 40s to put in approximately $100,000 a year tax-free; owners in their 50s to put in $200,000 a year; and those in their 60s and 70s up to $300,000 a year.[1]

Then we created a Roth 401(k) for the business, which lets them sock away $ 19,000 a year until they are 50, and $25,000 a year[2] after that. A Roth is paid for with after-tax dollars and grows tax-free, as there is no tax on withdrawals.

The final piece was a $500,000 10-Pay life insurance policy, on which they pay premiums for 10 years, but can then take out as much as $30,000 a *month*[3] in tax-free loans when they need the money, after 10 years of payments.

All this is perfectly legal—in fact, it's encouraged, and it trimmed Ray and Helen's tax bills while assuring them plenty of retirement income.

A special case? Not at all.

MEET OSCAR AND ANGIE

Oscar and Angie are doctors. He's a neurosurgeon and she is a general practitioner. They came to me with a massive tax problem. They hadn't thought about retirement and were paying large amounts of income tax on their earnings. Oscar worked at a hospital, but Angie owned her own practice.

First, we maxed out Oscar's 401(k), putting away $25,000 since he's just turned 51. Angie encouraged her head of human resources to adopt a cash-balance pension plan at age 52, so she put away $200,000 a year. That's a $224,500 reduction in taxable income!

They came to me stressed out, and now they're saving money for retirement and getting a big-time tax savings.

In recent years, there have been several critiques slamming the 401(k) and tax-deferred retirement savings vehicles like the 403(b), 457, and IRA. While I agree that some people shouldn't over-defer and put too much into tax-deferred savings at the exclusion of tax-free savings vehicles like Roths and cash-value insurance, those who save a lot in tax-deferred vehicles may wind up paying a lot of tax after they retire. But in the case of Angie and Oscar, they didn't have millions saved in tax-deferred vehicles. The deferred tax trap is something to worry about only if you are in a low tax bracket now (say 12 percent) and are deferring to a much higher bracket in the future. You generally need north of a considerable amount in tax-deferred plans (north of one million) before you need to worry.

We are not against retirement plans or against deferred tax plans *per se*. We are against blindly maxing out your 401(k) with no regard for the deferred tax trap.

Taxes, in fact, are the biggest problem with your 401(k) or IRA that you haven't thought about.

That's because, over time and history, tax rates tend to drift higher. Even if tax rates aren't higher when you retire, deductions may be fewer. Even if all goes according to plan and you become a 401(k) millionaire or hundred-thousandaire, once you turn 70½ you will have to deal with taxation at a compounded level. Every withdrawal will have federal and state income tax taken out. On top of that, your provisional income will go up, and you will have to pay taxes on up to 85 percent of your Social Security income. Then, when you die, federal or state death taxes will apply if you have a significant estate.

I am not saying to *not* contribute to a deferred tax savings vehicle: I am saying to contribute *with the end in mind*, as Stephen Covey once said. Don't do anything because I or some talking head tells you to.

Model out your strategies. In our era of cheap and no-fee funds or advice, don't be so cheap as to not pay for a planner to run these strategies out. A good financial planner is worth his or her weight in gold. Run a tax planning model first to see how your life would be affected in real life with your real tax brackets. If tax rates go up or if we even have lower rates but fewer deductions, you will thank me.

MEET PATRICK

Patrick is a big, gruff former law enforcement officer who had amassed $1 million, which he thought, not unreasonably, would let him retire comfortably and look after his teenage daughter. He entrusted his cash to an advisor at a local bank in New Jersey, who managed to turn $1 million in 1999 into $500,000 in 2002. The advisor wasn't a crook; he was just following the market down.

By staying in the market, Patrick saw his nest egg grow back to $750,000 by 2007. But the 2008 crash drove his savings back down to $500,000. That's two massive downswings in a decade!

"I'm *done* with the market," Patrick would growl at anybody who would listen.

Patrick is an ultraconservative investor (and gun fancier) whose biggest concern was that all his money go to his daughter, whom he had raised by himself. He had never had a big stomach for the stock market, having seen a $1 million nest egg shrink by half in two market downturns. He had even less of a stomach for his money going to the government in taxes.

For the first 10 years of his retirement, he chose to spend down his IRA money to zero by liquidating said IRA and using the funds to buy a unique type of permanent insurance, a dividend-paying participating permanent life insurance policy. He was the owner and the insured, and his daughter was the beneficiary. The policy is in his name, and she'll be well protected, just as Patrick wants. Meanwhile, his tax-deferred assets have decumulated conservatively, and he's achieved his goal of no more required minimum distributions from his IRAs at the end of the 10 years.

The US Tax Code is a sprawling, ever-changing mass of rules and regulations, which nevertheless contains dozens and dozens of provisions that can help you retire with more cash and less worry. Like most things to do with taxes and the law, they usually have weird names and weirder acronyms—what I call the alphabet soup of investing.

Some tax provisions are best taken advantage of before you retire, as you begin assembling your volatility buffer, consider new revenue streams, and figure out how best to invest your money.

The central idea: you've already paid tax on all or most of your income, so why pay tax *again* on your retirement savings if you don't have to?

Below are 10 great ways to minimize taxes once you've reached the age of 70½, and nearly all of them involve acting *now* rather than waiting until you've retired. I can't emphasize this enough. Millennials, get going! Generations X, Y, and boomers? Do this now if you haven't already!

You're not going to be able to do most of these yourself. Consider this chapter a guidepost to discuss with your financial advisor. He or she may find that some of these don't fit your exact situation. But if you have never heard of one or more of them, maybe you should find another advisor.

In brief, they are:

1. Pick out the right retirement savings vehicle for you (consider a cash balance pension).
2. Take out a Qualified Longevity Annuity Contract (QLAC).
3. Consider life insurance.

4. Incorporate yourself.
5. Form a C-Corp.
6. Buy an IRA condo using cost segregation.
7. Take advantage of the Qualified Charitable Distribution (QCD).
8. Get a part-time job at a charity.
9. Create a Charitable Remainder Unitrust (CRUT).
10. Manage your Required Minimum Distribution (RMD).
11. Turn a hobby into a business for the 20 percent Trump tax code self-employed write-off, known as the QBI deduction.

In a bit more detail, they are:

1. **Pick out the retirement savings vehicle for you.**
   This is one of the most important actions anyone can take, and it leads to all the other tips. Consider maxing out your 401(k) contributions, including allowable catch-ups, or maxing out your pension plan contributions. The tax laws in certain cases allow you to defer taxes on up to 100 percent of your annual income. It's great to do this if you have other assets, coming from money that's already been taxed that you can live on while your income grows tax-deferred. Doing this requires designing an individual retirement plan, in conjunction with your advisor. This should start during your first conversation with your advisor, depending on your age or circumstances. Possibilities include a company 401(k), a solo 401(k) if you're a small-business owner, a 401(k) with profit sharing, a cash balance pension plan, or a Roth IRA to take advantage of all legal ways to minimize your tax bill when you retire.

2.   **Take out a Qualified Longevity Annuity Contract (QLAC).**

The tax code allows you to put up to $125,000 in a Quality Longevity Annuity Contract, which charges no fees and protects your money against taxes that will be charged when you turn 70½ and are required to take a certain percentage of your IRA or 401(k) money. Required Minimum Distributions can be deferred until age 85 using the QLA. It protects you from running out of money, as the QLAC will give you an income for life and—bonus—keeps a chunk of your money out of your taxable income. This is one of many things you can do *now* to make life richer when you retire.

3.   **Consider life insurance.**

Yes, boring old vanilla life insurance, not universal life, not term life. These are policies that pay dividends and are issued by mutual companies, which mean they are owned by their policyholders. That means they are very conservative in how they manage your money. Most do not realize that insurance companies diversify your money using the most elite bond-management firms in the world. Your advisor should shop at least three different policies for you to make sure you are getting the best deal. A life insurance policy is a great way to hedge not only the volatility of the market but also the uncertainty of rising taxes now and in retirement. If you have a portfolio divided 60 percent in stocks and 40 percent in bonds, you could take the 40 percent that's in bonds and buy life insurance. You get a comparable rate of return as some bond funds, but you also get principal protection (the face value never goes down), money goes tax-free to your heirs when you die, and the IRS doesn't care about this money! It also has an added benefit that few people consider: for most policies, the insurance company will pay your premiums if you become disabled through what is called the Waiver of Premium rider.

4. **Incorporate yourself.**

Let's say you're nearing retirement, ready to leave that 9-to-5 job. The tax code allows you a key benefit, the creation of your Limited Liability Corporation, or LLC. There are ads all over TV for websites that offer to form one for you. Your legal advisor can do it in less than an hour. It just means incorporating yourself to do something you enjoy: freelance writing, being a travel agent if you enjoy traveling, being a horticultural advisor if you like gardening. Under the recently passed tax rules, certain LLCs can legally avoid taxes on 20 percent of their income through what is called a pass-through. Consult your advisor on this one: rules can change quickly.

5. **Form a C-Corp.**

This is a variation of forming an LLC. A C-Corporation is simply a normal company, taxed separately from you as the owner. It can be your hobby yarn business or your consulting company, or virtually anything else. One of the main reasons to do this, instead of doing the LLC mentioned above, is that in many cases the company can pay for your long-term-care insurance and write this off as a business expense. It's worth asking your advisor whether it's a good idea for you. If it is, you can save a lot of money while getting future health expenses covered.

6. **Buy an IRA condo using cost segregation.**
    Let's say you've always wanted to buy that second house and you're approaching retirement but still working. You could pull money out of your IRA to buy an investment property through something called cost segregation. Any advisor can show you how to do this. One strategy is to take a distribution from your personal IRA, normally taxable, and then loan that money to your LLC. Your LLC can then use those funds to buy a property, maybe a mixed-use multi-family dwelling, or a building occupied by your small business, or even a vacation home. The rules allow you to potentially use cost segregation to write off 20–30 percent of the purchase price of that home. Say you take out a $500,000 mortgage at 4 percent interest. That $20,000 of interest may get you only a $10,000 deduction under new tax rules, but you get to use or rent out the second house.

7. **Take advantage of the Qualified Charitable Distribution (QCD).**
    This one comes into its own once you've reached age 70½ and must take the Required Minimum Distributions from your 401(k) or IRA. Since these are taxable, they can easily bump you into a higher bracket if you've got Social Security (also taxable) or dividend or interest earnings, the total of which can also affect things like how much you pay for Medicare. Virtually

every retiree I see gripes about this requirement, and many take out the money, put it in their checking account, and pay taxes on the full amount on April 15. But there is a legal way to avoid part or all of this tax. One way is the Qualified Charitable Deduction. Under a QCD, you direct you IRA custodian (for example, Fidelity) to send your Required Minimum Distributions to the charity of your choice directly from your IRA in the amount of the Required Minimum Distribution. You get the tax deduction, and since the income never reaches you, you don't owe any taxes on it. It's fiddly, but important. As the ads for prescription drugs declare on TV, ask your advisor if this is right for you.

8. **Get a part-time job at a charity.**
    If you've already retired and love volunteering at the library, food pantry, or church, consider proposing that they employ you part-time. This can be a tax-efficient use of the funds the charity might get from donors or the government, and it can also make tax sense for you. It involves a type of retirement savings plan called a 403(b). Say you get a $24,000 yearly salary from the charity. You can put part or all of this directly into a 403(b) plan that works just like a 401(k). You don't pay any tax until you take it out.

9. **Create a Charitable Remainder Unitrust (CRUT).**
    Say that you were prescient enough to buy 10,000 shares of Apple stock at $5 a share in the early 1990s. Say you were also smart enough to just hold on to it. That stock is now worth about $180 a share, or about $1.8 million.

Great! Happy retirement! But you don't really want to pay income tax on a $1.8 million capital gain, do you? One solution for a highly appreciated asset, like that Apple stock, is to create a Charitable Remainder Unitrust. This involves setting up a trust for a charity, depositing the asset, and getting, say, a 5–7 percent payout a year for life. You'd pay taxes on the income, but you also get a whopping tax deduction based on the full value of the asset. It works for paintings, jewelry, antique cars, or stocks and funds that have gone way up in value since you bought or inherited it. As always, have your advisor explain this carefully to you before he or she sets it up.

10. **Manage your Required Minimum Distribution (RMD).**
The QCD is a good way to handle your required IRA distributions, but there are others. The required amount of money that you have to distribute from your 401(k) or IRA can be put into a cash-value life insurance policy, a long-term care policy, municipal bonds, or no-dividend stocks (think stocks like Berkshire that don't pay a dividend). That way you are not paying taxes twice on money you've already paid taxes on.

11. **Turn a hobby into a business.**
Paul and Tammy are a couple I know who are in the highest tax bracket of their life. They get pensions, Social Security, dividend, and annuity income. They have no child deduction, no mortgage deduction, and they don't own their convenience store anymore. What they love to do is make lamps and to travel. They set up an LLC for their lamp-making business, created

a nice website, and now travel all over the country exploring and living it up, from Long Beach, CA, to Long Beach Island, NJ, delivering lamps. It's a useful $25,000 yearly income and a great tax deduction. They can deduct expenses for lamp-making supplies, their home workshop, and car and hotel expenses on the road. They are happily seeing the USA on Uncle Sam's dime.

ACTION STEPS

- Be active in your tax planning. This can save you hundreds of thousands of dollars.
- Consult your advisor frequently to take advantage of changing tax rules.
- Don't be driven solely by tax considerations, but don't ignore them either.

TAKE CHARGE OF YOUR SITUATION TODAY

Let's see how this all works.

To get started, take our free assessment at retirementrealitycheck .com. Then answer the self-assessment questions that follow. These exercises serve the purpose of giving you not only information, but hope. Armed with these questions and answers, and with the tools presented in the rest of this book, you should be able to work with a financial advisor to change your life. And if your advisor doesn't want to do some things you find sensible—find another advisor who will.

SELF-ASSESSMENT

1. **How do you feel about your financial situation?**
    a. Comfortable
    b. Uneasy
    c. Worried
    d. Scared
    e. Terrified

2. **How would you characterize your knowledge of personal finance, investment, and savings choices?**
    a. Minuscule
    b. I know a bit but want to know more
    c. I'm an expert at some things, shaky about others
    d. I'm a total ace

3. **When it comes to your risk comfort level, are you more inclined to go after a sure thing or a maybe?**
    a. Sure thing
    b. Maybe

4. **Do you work with a financial advisor?**
    a. Never
    b. I did but gave up on him/her
    c. Yes, but unhappily
    d. Yes, happily

5. How much money do you have specifically saved for your retirement?
   a. $0–$100,000
   b. $100,000–$500,000
   c. $500,000–$1,000,000
   d. $1,000,000–$10,000,000

6. How much money do you have saved for an emergency?
   a. Nothing
   b. $100–$10,000
   c. $10,000–50,000
   d. $50,000–$100,000
   e. $100,000–$250,000
   f. >$250,000

7. How much do you think you'll need for retirement?
   a. $100,000
   b. $500,000
   c. $1 million
   d. $5 million
   e. No clue

8. How much money do you save each month after paying all your bills?
   a. $0–$500
   b. $500–$1,000
   c. >$1,000

9. About how much credit-card debt do you carry over each month?
   a. Zero
   b. Between $1 and $999
   c. >$1,000

10. Do you have insurance that would cover a disability that caused you to miss work?
    a. Yes
    b. No

11. **If you have kids between 6 months and 15 years old, how much have you saved for each one's education?**
    a. Nothing
    b. $50,000
    c. $100,000
    d. >$100,000

12. **Do you have life insurance?**
    a. No
    b. Yes, a term policy from work
    c. Yes, a whole-life policy

13. **Do you have any income that doesn't come from a salary?**
    a. No
    b. Yes, from a savings account
    c. Yes, from stocks and bonds
    d. Yes, from an annuity
    e. Yes, from part-time work

14. **Do you have a 401(k), IRA, or Roth IRA?**
    a. Yes, I contribute a little whenever I can
    b. Yes, I max out every week
    c. I think so, but I'm not sure
    d. What's a 401(k)?

15. **If you could have 20 percent more income a month, what would you do with it?**
    a. Pay off my credit cards
    b. Save it
    c. Go out to dinner more often
    d. Give more to charity
    e. Take a vacation

3

REALITY CHECK

BUY TERM LIFE INSURANCE AND INVEST THE DIFFERENCE VS. BUY WHOLE AND INVEST THE REST.

MEET JIM AND PATTI

I met Jim, a government employee, at a seminar when the Dow hit 6,666 in March 2008. He was rightfully concerned about the state of the stock market, but he had a deeper question: How should he take his pension? So, after a rousing talk, he brought his wife to an initial consult we did for seminar attendees the next Saturday at my office in Bordentown, NJ.

While Jim was looking for a way to maximize the benefits of the government pension he and Patti (who also worked for the state) had earned, she wasn't on board at all. She sat there grim-faced, fists clenched, arms drawn across her chest. Whatever I was advising, she wasn't complying. She continually appealed to talking heads on the TV and radio that were denying what I was saying. If I'd said the sky was blue, she would have told me it was red. Defeatedly, I got in my car and cried all the way back to my little row home. Mind you, it was a Saturday. I worked on a non-work day for this prospective client. I thought I had failed. . . .

But before I tell you how we overcame Patti's initial objections to our strategy, let's look at the strategy she had first: BTID, or Buy Term, Invest the Difference. This strategy, popularized by Dave Ramsey and others, says that cash-value life insurance is a rip-off; according to him, you'd be better off investing the money you spent on whole life and buy mutual funds that return more.

On the surface, this strategy might make sense, if we lived in an ideal world:

> A world with . . .
> No taxes
> No fees
> No risk
> No disability
> No long-term-care illness
> No early demise

Fat chance!

Let's look at what would really happen (see chart, top of the next page):

The ideal investment that makes 9 percent—hardly the 12 percent that Ramsey and his ilk claim—would be taxed, and you would have to pay fees for advice coupled with term insurance costs. All of this assumes you never get disabled, never die, and never have a loss in your ability to save $10,000 every year like clockwork.

	AVERAGE RETURN	NET RETURN	DIFFERENTIAL	NET RESULT
	7.03%	**5.14%**	**$65,112**	**$299,830**

YEAR	BALANCE B.O.Y	RATE OF RETURN	ANNUAL PAYMENT	ANNUAL TERM	TOTAL FEES	ANNUAL TAX	BALANCE E.O.Y
[1] 2000	$0	(-9.10%)	$10,000	(-$2,000)	(-$91)	$0	$8,999
[2] 2001	$8,999	(-11.89%)	$10,000	(-$2,000)	(-$167)	$0	$16,573
[3] 2002	$16,573	(-22.1%)	$10,000	(-$2,000)	(-$207)	$0	$20,493
[4] 2003	$20,493	28.68%	$10,000	(-$2,000)	(-$373)	(-$1,934)	$36,932
[5] 2004	$36,932	10.88%	$10,000	(-$2,000)	(-$509)	(-$1,129)	$50,400
[6] 2005	$50,400	4.91%	$10,000	(-$2,000)	(-$627)	(-$656)	$62,083
[7] 2006	$62,083	15.97%	$10,000	(-$2,000)	(-$809)	(-$2,517)	$80,139
[8] 2007	$80,139	5.49%	$10,000	(-$2,000)	(-$940)	(-$1,094)	$93,053
[9] 2008	$93,053	(-37.00%)	$10,000	(-$2,000)	(-$649)	$0	$64,274
[10] 2009	$64,274	26.46%	$10,000	(-$2,000)	(-$896)	(-$4,345)	$88,686
[11] 2010	$88,686	15.06%	$10,000	(-$2,000)	(-$1,103)	(-$3,286)	$109,160
[12] 2011	$109,160	2.11%	$10,000	(-$2,000)	($1,211)	(-$556)	$119,907
[13] 2012	$119,907	16.00%	$10,000	(-$2,000)	($1,461)	(-$4,596)	$144,635
[14] 2013	$144,635	32.39%	$10,000	(-$2,000)	($1,936)	(-$11,074)	$191,711
[15] 2014	$191,711	13.69%	$10,000	(-$2,000)	($2,232)	(-$6,106)	$220,988
[16] 2015	$220,988	1.38%	$10,000	(-$2,000)	($2,335)	(-$705)	$231,136
[17] 2016	$231,136	11.96%	$10,000	(-$2,000)	($2,636)	(-$6,376)	$260,963
[18] 2017	$260,963	21.83%	$10,000	(-$2,000)	(-$3,170)	(-$13,078)	$313,866
					Deferred Taxes	(-$14,036)	
Totals			**$180,000**	(-$36,000)	(-$21,354)	(-$71,487)	**$299,830**

All of this represents a loss of nearly $128,841 in taxes, fees, and the term insurance costs combined. When this couple retired, they would not be able to maximize their pension because they would no longer have the death benefit. The term insurance would have expired; therefore Patti would have had to take a reduced pension in order to protect her husband if she died before him.

This brings us to the major BTID flaws: it assumes we will never be taxed, never have a long-term illness, never desire or need a death benefit; it assumes our contribution amount will be constant and that we will never want to maximize our pensions if we have them.

Patti came to believe in our process because of the flaws inherent in the BTID strategy.

I also want to remind you of the danger of listening to talking heads on the TV.

Social proof is powerful for us human beings, as we are inherently social. Even though talking heads may bad-mouth what I'm about to share with you, there are just as many brilliant people doing what I'm about to share.

SOCIAL PROOF #1
ELITE COLLEGE COACHES

What do Dabo Swinney of Clemson, Jim Harbaugh of Michigan, and Dawn Staley of the University of South Carolina all have in common?[1]

They are choosing to take massive bonuses in the form of life insurance. One of the reasons many of you haven't heard of or considered cash-value life insurance may be the negative things said about it by the likes of famous financial talking heads. It is important to note that some ill-conceived life insurance strategies may not be the best for you. These include policies with a rising cost of insurance, or policies without guaranteed cash value. The media moguls are often guilty of the straw-man fallacy. Do you remember that logical fallacy from high school or college? That's where you create an opposing argument that really isn't true. These media types paint their opposing view in such a negative way that no one wants to buy it.

Let me remind you of what you may have said to your kids or grandkids: just because everyone is doing it doesn't make it right. Be very wary of talking heads denigrating something when they haven't carefully weighed all options. Just as there may be social proof against life insurance, there is a rising tide of many who desire to keep some of their assets off the radar of the IRS and are now considering cash-value life insurance.

The latest craze is for college coaches to be given payment in the form of split-dollar life cash-value life insurance policies.

If it's good enough for elite college coaches, it may be worth reconsidering.

SOCIAL PROOF #2
COLI OR CORPORATE-OWNED LIFE INSURANCE: DO WHAT SUZE'S EMPLOYERS DO, NOT WHAT SHE SAYS

Barry Dyke's *Pirates of Manhattan II* details at length Suze Orman's continual hostility against permanent life insurance. In Suze's book *The Money Book for the Young, Fabulous and Broke*, she decries permanent life insurance and only promotes level term. She talks about even hating whole life. "The only life insurance I like is term life insurance."

Suze's employers don't do what she says. Neither should you. Suze's show airs on CNBC. Comcast now owns CNBC. Mind you, I appreciate Suze's message of empowering women for financial success. She is clear, concise, and compelling, but she's not infallible. Former CEO of Comcast Ralph Roberts had over $215 million in cash value in life insurance at the time of his death.[2] Current Comcast CEO Brian Roberts has nearly $223 million in a policy. Now, I am not saying you should run out and buy a life insurance policy just because her employers did. I am saying not to dismiss valid strategies just because they are demonized.

SOCIAL PROOF #3
BOLI, OR BANK-OWNED LIFE INSURANCE

TD Ameritrade is one of the major sponsors of Orman's program. Yet TD doesn't put their money in term insurance. In fact, they do quite the opposite. TD has $845 million in high cash-value life insurance. TD has more invested in life insurance than they do in the Boston Garden hockey arena. But it's not just TD; much of the banking industry believes in the power of life insurance to bolster its reserves.[3]

Motley Fool's "Math Guy," Matthew Frankel, refers to BOLI as "a little-known way that banks make money." Frankel elaborates the motivation for banks to include so much life insurance on their balance sheet: "BOLI policies produce far superior returns than traditional bank investments . . . and, the growth in the cash value of the policies, as well as any death benefits paid out, are completely tax-free."

According to the *Equias Alliance/Michael White Report*, BOLI assets were up 4 percent in 2017 to $168 billion.[4] The amount of Tier 1 capital that banks have is growing and is another proof that if it is good enough for banks, it may be good enough for you to not dismiss it as a potential option.

SOCIAL PROOF #4
TAX AND INCOME FINANCIAL PRACTITIONERS

Elite tax professionals and tax-conscious authors such as Ed Slott[5] and Tom Hegna lead a chorus of CPAs and financial industry veterans now calling for us to reevaluate permanent life insurance. Hegna details why he loves permanent life insurance in his latest book:

> Even if some retirees don't want to leave anything for their own children, they LOVE their grandchildren and can help provide for a college education or money for their first house. . . . Many retirees have philanthropic wishes and want to leave money to their church, university, or favorite charity. Life Insurance allows you to do that! . . . Use Life Insurance to replace retirement income that will cease at the death of a spouse, such as Social Security thus protecting your benefits!

We now know a new herd is brewing for the value of incorporating permanent life insurance into a financial plan. But we shouldn't do things just because public opinion is changing. You should do this because you and your advisor have explored it as something conforming to your objectives.

Here are 11 reasons Patti decided to buy a permanent life policy. They may change your mind about what the talking heads say about insurance. You may want to consider cash-value life insurance because of these benefits:

1. The death benefit obviously protects your family in the event of your early demise. We will all have final expenses. Funerals and health care cost money. We are all guaranteed to meet our Maker, so why not be prepared?

2. It's a permission slip to spend down assets in retirement. I get some people who want to spend as much of their money as possible, but they are afraid to because their assets become their insurance policy at death (they self-insure). If you have a life insurance policy for your spouse and kids, you can spend all of your money before you die. And at your funeral, the last check can even bounce as the hearse drives off. Your heirs get the insurance payout.

3. Life insurance offers protection from creditors for your estate. This is true in many states.

4. Disability protection with Waiver of Premium in the event of disability.

5. Forced Savings Plan, also known as the tin-can effect. It allows you to put savings on autopilot via automatic deduction.

6. College planning. The insurance doesn't count against you as an asset when you apply for financial aid at your kids' colleges. The FAFSA (Federal Application for Federal Student Aid) doesn't count it.

7. Tax-advantaged—it's like a Roth on steroids. Do you believe taxes will go up, or down, in the future? I don't know about you, but with ever-increasing government debt and unfunded liabilities in Social Security and Medicare, I see taxes possibly going up. I believe the next few years of the Trump tax code—regardless of how you may feel about it—present a rare window of opportunity: pay taxes now at lower rates and reposition assets to tax-smart vehicles like life insurance and Roths. Many people don't truly understand the power of tax-exempt vehicles. Municipal bonds are tax-free but aren't totally tax-exempt, because municipal bond income counts as provisional income for the taxation of

Social Security. Meanwhile, life insurance loans don't hurt you.

8. To borrow on an asset that is increasing and still getting dividends, even if you borrow money for college or spending needs.

9. Comparative yield—or, as CPA Bryan Bloom puts it, "Capital Equivalent Value (CEV)." What is CEV? It's a term to denote what an asset would need to generate to garner a similar net yield. In *Confessions of a CPA*, he describes the yield one would have to get in the market in order for the market-based asset to produce a similar net yield. When people focus on the rate of return of life insurance, they may be disappointed. However, when we focus on what we need to make in a tax-free environment in order to generate a similar yield, then cash-value life insurance could be deemed a superior vehicle for your spending and enjoying years. Realize the life insurance is not predominantly an accumulation strategy to build wealth (your assets, stocks, funds, and income should do that). Rather, it is a superior distribution technique.

Remember what the Mount Everest climbers said? The riskiest part is not the ascent (akin to your working years), but rather the descent (your retirement distribution years). If you don't get down the mountain safely, all the growth was for naught. A lot of people are focused on growth of their assets. That's good, but you should be focused on distribution as well.

a. This may be the biggest new reason to do life insurance, because it answers the question of where you should put your money. The key question is: *Where should I put my money compared to what?*

b. Life insurance has a mediocre internal rate of return. It's not about rate of return, but about the rate of distribution. After 10 years, the cash value may be a little less or more than what you contributed, but try to find another product with a better tax-free yield.

c. For example, a 55-year-old purchases a 10-Pay whole-life policy (he pays premiums for 10 years) and puts in $100,000 per year. At the end of 10 years, it's a low rate of return. We have to think of the value we are getting from the asset. So, what's the value of this asset? This person can take out as retirement income over $67,000 tax-free in distributions from age 65 through age 90, according to a current dividend scale from a leading life insurance company. All this with a death benefit of $600K at age 90. $67K times 25 years is $1.6 million. And add the death benefit (DB). Total benefit is $2,337,000. This is huge, because if one compares the life insurance to the traditional buy-and-hold, that $100,000 per year in the stock market would have had to grow by 11.54 percent just to beat the insurance. That may work in a bull market, but you'd have to have nerves of steel and never sell your equities.

d. Formula: Payout (P)/safe withdrawal rate = the amount you would need to replace the life insurance. P = 67,000 divided by 3.5 percent equals 1,914,285.71. Realize this isn't saying the rate of return is 11.54 percent: it's saying that for you to beat the payout of the life insurance, you would need to make the 11.54 percent tax-free.

e. Then he talks taxes. If you are in a taxable IRA or 401(k), you'd need 14.37 percent to beat the life insurance. Now, when we say beat the life insurance, we are not talking about rate of return; we are talking the yield necessary to equate to.

Tax Rate	CEV	ROR
15%	$2,252,100	14.37%
25%	$2,552,380	16.55%
40%	$3,190,475	20.41%

f. Who is getting 11.54 percent tax-free every year? Answer: no one. That makes the 10-Pay so compelling as a retirement income tool. Now, I want to be clear, the actual rate of return on the cash value is not 11.54. But that's what you would have needed to make in the market at a 3.5 percent distribution rate to tie the insurance.

10. No equity market risk. Never check the Dow again!

11. Pension maximization. This is the strategy Patti and Pete seized for their benefit. Because of the presence of the death benefit from the life insurance policy, Patti could leave her husband the life insurance and take the highest "life only" pension option. The benefit of the "life only" option is higher income. The negative is that it would disinherit Pete of the pension. However, Pete was okay with getting no pension, because the pension would be taxable but the life insurance death benefit would be tax-free from state and federal income taxes.

Now Patti is a dear client, and she and Pete are relaxing in retirement. How did we change her from skeptic to believer? We showed her the power of social proof and the 11 reasons to consider insurance. It didn't hurt either that her friend told her that our pension maximization strategy using life insurance was a good idea.

What we did for Pete and Patti was set up a spend-down strategy to make their pension dollars gain greater potential interest than if they'd just put them in a bank account. Even though it's a way to accumulate savings, it's really a spend-down strategy because the timing and way you withdraw money and spend it can make your money go much further than you'd expect.

We used a volatility buffer to give them some optionality. We set up a cash-value life policy that would eventually let them borrow against it to pay for their kids' college educations, avoiding a 529 savings plan, which they would have had to declare when they applied for financial aid. With this strategy, Patti and Pete, who own a vacation house in the Pocono Mountains, were able to send their two boys to college on in-state tuition without making a dent in their long-term savings.

Using spend-down strategies like this has allowed Pete and Patti to fund college and wind up with about $800,000 in savings and insurance, up from about $500,000 when we met 10 years ago.

Advisors should help clients find the right spend-down vehicles and encourage them to forget about them until they need them. That's what Patti and Pete did and they are clients of mine to this day.

ACTION STEPS

- Seriously consider the right type of life insurance.
- Develop a conservative spend-down strategy.

REALITY CHECK

ANNUITIES AREN'T THE DEVIL: THEY CAN DELIVER 30 PERCENT MORE INCOME IN RETIREMENT. ANNUITIES ARE YOUR FRIEND.

THINK ABOUT IT. WHO ACTUALLY HATES THEIR PENSION?

I live in New Jersey, where teachers typically retire on a nice pension (called the NJ Teachers Pension and Annuity Fund) of $30,000–$60,000 every year. I have never heard them complain about the rate of return on their pension. They love getting consistent checks every month, without fear of their money going down due to stock market volatility. In fact, politicians have even derided them unfairly due to the envy that exists for that stable monthly income. Although many well-qualified teachers endured a lower salary for 30 to 40 years, town halls were being held and envy stoked because they were getting a steady annuity. Now, I know not everyone likes an annuity, but have you ever heard of a pensioner who refused a check? I've heard of retirees decrying fortunes lost in an index fund but never heard a complaint about a pension. They usually wished their monthly paycheck was greater.

WHAT IS AN ANNUITY?

Since many people can't buy a pension, they opt for the next best thing: an annuity. An annuity is a savings account with an insurance company. An annuity is a broad category much like buying a car. Thousands of annuities exist—some good, some not so good. Most allow for an option for income guaranteed for life. An annuity is a way for you to develop a spending plan and spend all your money without running out of income. It is essentially like you buying your own pension. The guarantees are based on the claims-paying ability of an underlying insurance company. Generally, you want an annuity from a company with a rating of A– or higher, according to a reputable ratings guide like AM Best or Standard and Poor's. Before you dismiss all annuities as bad, read on for an interesting innovation in annuity design.

MEET ALAN AND ASHLEY

Alan, whom we met earlier, is a 74-year-old ramrod-straight, thin, ex–Bell Labs engineer trying to enjoy retirement at a gated community in central New Jersey with his wife, Ashley. They own their house outright and their two kids are grown, but Alan was anxious.

Ten years ago, Alan was a mess. He weighed 35 pounds more than he does today. He went to every investment seminar offered at his active adult community, trying to figure out how to invest the $600,000 he had saved so he and his wife could retire comfortably. All those seminars reinforced his distrust of investment advisors as a class. He watched CNBC every day and surfed the web for investment advice. He checked his portfolio of dividend-paying stocks eight times a day, especially one stock—a Nasdaq-traded real estate investment trust that reached a high of almost $25 a share before it lost nearly half its value. His idea—to buy high-yield stocks and retire on the dividends of nearly 7 percent a year—didn't work, and he got hammered by the 2008 crash. He had a system, but it wasn't necessarily working. He analyzed every financial decision according to the system. In 2011, when Ashley saw a bargain house in Florida available at the bottom of the market, they didn't pull the trigger because the investment didn't fit into Alan's system. You could see the regret in her eyes, but she was too sweet to disparage her husband in front of me.

As with several of my other clients, it took Alan about six meetings before he agreed to hire me. I had given him my home address and later found he had driven out to see what sort of house I lived in, to see if I was a man of substance. He'd gotten the address wrong and couldn't find the house, leading to some confusion. One day he called me and said, "Hey, Josh, there is no house at this address." I replied, "Alan, you inverted the house number, and why again are you stalking me?" So far as I can tell, he's the only client I've ever had that stalked me.

By the end of our sixth meeting, Ashley, her eyes puffy from anxiety and her shoulders weighed down with worry, said: "Alan, if you don't sign with Josh right now, I'm leaving."

He signed. She stayed. They are living happily ever after.

Here's how we did it: the often-maligned annuity.

Now, part of the reason Alan took six meetings to understand everything was because he thought annuities were the Rodney Dangerfield of investments, as Jane Bryant Quinn puts it. Jane Bryant Quinn is a leading financial commentator and bestselling author of *How To Make Your Money Last: The Indispensable Retirement Guide*. Annuities get no respect, and Alan wasn't ready to give them any consideration due to the negatives he'd heard about. However, even the likes of Quinn are giving annuities a second look. She now offers glowing praise for certain no-fee annuities.[1]

I'D RATHER DIE AND "GO TO HELL" THAN BUY AN ANNUITY

While Quinn joins a growing chorus of those who see the good in annuities, Ken Fisher would rather face eternal damnation than buy an annuity. I personally find him a brilliant marketer; but this statement by the famous investment guru offends me. One, it takes matters of spiritual destiny too lightly. Two, it undermines a valid retirement strategy that has attracted more than $1 trillion in the last few years. Annuities are often seen as the redheaded stepchildren of investing.

Why does this investment player hate annuities so much? Because annuities have grown more popular. Fee-based advisors are beginning to take notice because they are losing revenue due to annuities rising in popularity. If we use 1.25 percent as the average fee for the $1 trillion, then the Wall Street–centered advisors (who prefer stocks, bonds, and ETFs over annuities) are losing over $12.5 billion a year in fees. That's one reason asset undermanagement-based advisors hate them: lost revenue.

But Ken Fisher doesn't hate *all* annuities. He loves his own annuity—his clients. These prognosticators who say they hate annuities prove they love them in how they get paid. Think about it. By last count, Fisher managed an astronomical $90 billion. A fee of 1.25 percent on that $90 billion is an astonishing $1.125 billion that he makes off clients in fees every year—regardless of performance. He gets an annuity of $1.125 billion every year. There's nothing wrong with that: God bless him for success.

But why is an annuity good enough for him but not you? I don't think these sorts of advisors are necessarily in it for selfish reasons. He probably believes that he can grow assets better than an annuity. Maybe he can, or maybe he can't. It doesn't matter. People should buy annuities for protection, not growth. Perhaps these advisors exclude a whole category of product just because it doesn't fit with their compensation model.

Meanwhile, Fisher and other annuity haters love investing in companies that promote them. For several years, based on his SEC filings, he disclosed that he had a large investment in American Equity Investment Life Insurance Company. They are one of the largest marketers of fixed-indexed annuities in the country.

Other famous gurus talk smack about annuities. They claim that they can do what an annuity can do, only cheaper. But how? Utilizing bond ETFs. I will go into bonds in great detail later, but it is very difficult for bonds to behave like annuities in this interest-rate environment. To be sure, in the 1980s and 1990s, when government bonds were paying much higher rates, the average person didn't need an annuity, because bond yields were so good. But if we look at two common bond funds used by those who promote bonds to the exclusion of annuities, we see that a simple 3 percent to 4 percent fixed annuity outperformed many bond funds over the last five years. For the last five years, Morningstar shows that the five-year average for ultrashort, short-term government debt, short-term, and intermediate bond funds was approximately 1.76 percent (Fund Category Performance: Total Returns 2019). Now, history doesn't repeat and all that jazz, but an annuity is a tool, just like a bond. I would hate to throw the baby out with the bathwater.

For whatever reason, there is a whole lot of antiannuity fever out there. The giant retirement company TIAA-CREF found in a recent study that 84 percent of those surveyed want a guaranteed monthly income, but only 14 percent want to buy an annuity.

In effect, 84 percent of retirees want annuities, but only 14 percent buy them. I suspect that's got something to do with stigma and terminology. It's sort of like people who oppose government health insurance but love Medicare.

Why buy an annuity?

1. Income
2. Principal Protection
3. Conservative Growth
4. Long-Term-Care Provision

YOUR ANNUITY STINKS!

Soon after my friend Benjamin bought an annuity, everyone told him it stunk. He bought it in 2004. When we got together, we looked at the fine print, because he was troubled as to why his former advisor—whom he considered a friend—would have put him in such a bad product. So, we gave the contract a closer look. He put in $100,000 in 2004. Guess how much he had in his rider in 2019? The minimum guarantee would have been over $300,000 for income purposes. That would be the equivalent of having 7 percent compounded per year. Too bad he canceled the annuity due to peer pressure.

ALAN'S SOLUTION

The solution for Alan was to reposition about $600,000 of his assets. After the 2008 market crash, we sold his stock and put the proceeds into a variety of vehicles, including a fixed-index annuity and a reverse mortgage. The conservative assets he was in didn't grow nearly as much as the stock market did in subsequent years (although Alan's favorite stock still went nowhere), but the income is adequate, and the worry is gone.

The annuity generates an income of $30,000 per year for life, according to the income rider, and the reverse mortgage also generates about $30,000 a year. The couple gets $40,000 a year from Social Security, for a total income of $100,000. It's secure. It's enough. A SWAN—sleep well at night—plan.

Now at age 74, Alan has never looked better, and has the energy and time to take runs around the community. He and Ashley are ever-smiling, taking a trip to Naples, Florida, here, and a Colorado skiing vacation there. They are enjoying life, and Alan has stopped watching CNBC, the anxiety all gone.

Very often, transitioning to a conservative posture can mean getting your life back.

How did this transformation happen?

RETHINK ANNUITIES

The key for Alan and Ashley was the much-maligned annuity. An annuity is simply a contract between you and a life insurance company that, in return for a lump-sum payment, you'll get income for a fixed period, similar to a pension, along with some other benefits. There are two main payouts, immediate and deferred, and four flavors of annuities.

Annuities are backed by at least four layers of protection. First, how the insurance company invests your money in an immediate, fixed, or fixed-indexed annuity. A life insurance company typically invests your annuity premium in their general reserve account—alongside with their own investments. They must follow Prudent Person Laws to invest the principal you give them in conservative investments like treasuries and investment-grade debt instruments. They typically invest 80–90 percent in high-quality bonds. Second, they must maintain sufficient reserves. Even if a company falls into trouble, they can't declare bankruptcy. Rather, they usually get bought out or stop selling new product. Third, they are heavily regulated by the states and special attention should be given to the solvency ratio. You want to make sure the solvency ratio of the annuity you pick is greater than 100 percent. The solvency ratio of an insurance company is the size of its capital relative to all the risk it has taken, which is all liabilities subtracted from total assets. In other words, solvency is a measurement of how much the company has in assets versus how much it owes. It is a basic measure of how financially sound an insurer is and its ability to pay claims. It helps investors measure the company's ability to meet its obligations and is similar to the capital adequacy ratio of banks. It is an indicator of the firm's long-term survival.

There are two types of payouts:

1. **Immediate:** You invest, let's say, $500,000 in an annuity that starts paying you a lump sum every month or every year for the rest of your life. A typical payout might be $2,500 a month. Some policies let you get paid immediately but limit the term to, say, five years, which might net you as much as $8,500 a month. In either case, the money is stuck—there are usually heavy penalties for early withdrawal, and there's no hedge against inflation. There are no fees, but you may have to pay tax on the

money you receive, and if you die before all your money gets paid back to you, the insurance company keeps the difference. I generally don't recommend these unless you really need the extra income.

2.   **Deferred:** You wait at least a year to start your payments, while the balance may grow or decline, though it does grow tax-deferred.

There are four general categories of annuities:

1.   **A fixed annuity:** This version is simple. You commit to a certain number of years. If you tie your money up for 5 years, you will receive 3 percent interest; tie it up for 10 years, and you get 3.9 percent. There are no internal fees, only a surrender charge if you take more than 10 percent a year out. Annuities usually offer higher rates than banks offer for the same length of time—3 years, 5 years, or 7 years, for example. These can be hedges against rising interest rates because when they mature you can roll your money into the new, higher-rate annuity if rates improve. When I recommend these types of annuities, I often suggest the investor ladder—that is, buy annuities with different maturity dates, to guard against interest-rate risk while still taking advantage of higher rates if they happen.

2.   **A fixed-indexed annuity:** This is sort of like the baby of a fixed annuity and an index fund. This kind protects your principal, and the interest rate you get is linked to an index that you choose. Keep in mind that the money isn't in the index, but interest is tied indirectly to it. So, if you think the stock market is still going to go up, you can pick the Standard & Poor's (S&P)

500 index, and if it goes up 10 percent you get a piece of that, called the participation rate. You don't get all the upside, but you have no loss of principal if the market tanks.

3. **A variable annuity:** This is as if a mutual fund and an insurance policy had a baby. Principal value fluctuates based on how well you do at picking mutual funds. There are many variations within this class, including those that let you pick investments from a menu every year, or, even more often, those that let you buy a rider that guarantees you a death benefit if the market tanks or an income benefit for income for life. Generally, these have higher fees but may offer more benefits.

4. **Immediate annuities:** These pay you a fixed amount right away, or you could get them in a DIA (Deferred Income Annuity). This is sort of like a pension. It'll bring you guaranteed income for life. There are no investment fees or commissions taken out of the immediate, fixed, or fixed-indexed annuity unless you add a rider. Keep in mind that the immediate may be irrevocable—meaning you could be stuck with that one for life. It's not necessarily bad to get a paycheck for life; just be aware it may not be something you can get out of.

As we'll see, matching the right type of annuity to the right investor can bring serenity and may reduce risk.

But matching provisions to need can be tricky, and all too often investors, acting on their own or in response to marketing solicitations or a free cruise or a whizz-bang seminar, wind up paying too much for an annuity that returns them too little and produces more angst than assurance. The key here: make sure an annuity is right for you before you buy it.

A HYPOTHETICAL ANNUITY ILLUSTRATED

I'm about to show you what these talking heads hate. In this example, a 60-year-old man who is forced to retire early came to me with a very real need—income. He could have done the traditional thing. But just think back to how he would have felt if all of his money had been in the S&P 500, like Warren Buffett famously proposed for his widow.

Think about how you would have felt going through two of the worst stock downturns in history, losing nearly 40 percent twice in one decade. In the illustrations provided on pages 80–82, the client put in $700,000 and is now able to take out nearly $35,527 per year for life due to the income rider on a fixed-indexed annuity. The safe distribution rate one year after purchasing this annuity is 4.9 percent—nearly 40 percent higher than the safe withdrawal rate many posit in our industry—3 percent from a traditionally diversified portfolio. All this without the Alka-Seltzer needed to endure a volatile market!

To understand the following charts, let's explain the terms. In these charts, this gentleman delays withdrawing money until the end of year two, when he's just turning 62. I included the interest the annuity company could have given him, which is less than the return on the S&P 500—but remember that when the market loses 11.82 percent in year three, his index credit is zero and his principal is protected. That's one reason to like a fixed as opposed to a variable annuity. The accumulation value refers to the amount he'd leave his heirs. Note that the insurance company doesn't take all his money at death. See the Legacy Planning column on page 82? When the investor is 80, there is still a death benefit.

Principal Protection & Growth Potential

Selected Period
1/1/1998 to 1/1/2018

End Of Year	Income	S&P 500 DRC 5% Index Change	S&P 500 Index Change	Accumulation Value	Allocated Interest Credited
At Issue				$700,000	
1	$0	9.41%	25.95%	$746,050	7.53%
2	$34,318	8.68%	18.49%	$755,884	7.20%
3	$35,527	1.09%	-11.82%	$714,076	0.12%
4	$35,527	-1.06%	-10.02%	$671,368	0.00%
5	$35,527	-4.58%	-21.27%	$628,368	0.00%
6	$35,527	8.37%	21.94%	$627,782	7.05%
7	$35,527	4.79%	8.44%	$615,993	5.22%
8	$35,527	4.13%	5.55%	$598,993	4.43%
9	$35,527	9.62%	11.65%	$599,520	7.67%
10	$35,527	4.81%	2.16%	$574,204	3.08%
11	$35,527	-4.43%	-35.61%	$531,479	0.00%
12	$35,527	6.04%	21.59%	$517,900	5.87%
13	$35,527	4.94%	12.51%	$500,829	5.31%
14	$35,527	-0.88%	0.41%	$459,076	0.21%
15	$35,527	4.53%	14.51%	$438,087	5.13%
16	$35,527	10.37%	25.27%	$427,775	8.05%
17	$35,527	4.26%	12.35%	$404,654	4.99%
18	$35,527	-2.06%	-2.21%	$361,946	0.00%
19	$35,527	4.52%	12.18%	$336,060	5.15%
20	$35,527	14.97%	19.40%	$324,300	10.30%
Total	$673,804			Average	4.37%
				Total Interest Earned	$441,089

Guaranteed Lifetime Income Benefit
(Showing values as of the next year)

End Of Year	Income	Age	Income Base	Lifetime Benefit Percentage	Lifetime Benefit Amount	Nursing Home Benefit
At Issue		60	$700,000	4.50%	$31,500	NA
1	$0	61	$746,050	4.60%	$34,318	NA
2	$34,318	62	$755,884	4.70%	$35,527	NA
3	$35,527	63	$755,884	4.70%	$35,527	NA
4	$35,527	64	$755,884	4.70%	$35,527	NA
5	$35,527	65	$755,884	4.70%	$35,527	$75,588
6	$35,527	66	$755,884	4.70%	$35,527	$75,588
7	$35,527	67	$755,884	4.70%	$35,527	$75,588
8	$35,527	68	$755,884	4.70%	$35,527	$75,588
9	$35,527	69	$755,884	4.70%	$35,527	$75,588
10	$35,527	70	$755,884	4.70%	$35,527	$75,588
11	$35,527	71	$755,884	4.70%	$35,527	$75,588
12	$35,527	72	$755,884	4.70%	$35,527	$75,588
13	$35,527	73	$755,884	4.70%	$35,527	$75,588
14	$35,527	74	$755,884	4.70%	$35,527	$75,588
15	$35,527	75	$755,884	4.70%	$35,527	$75,588
16	$35,527	76	$755,884	4.70%	$35,527	$75,588
17	$35,527	77	$755,884	4.70%	$35,527	$75,588
18	$35,527	78	$755,884	4.70%	$35,527	$75,588
19	$35,527	79	$755,884	4.70%	$35,527	$75,588
20	$35,527	80	$755,884	4.70%	$35,527	$75,588
Total	**$673,804**					

Selected Period
1/1/1998 to 1/1/2018

End Of Year	Income	Legacy Planning Guaranteed Death Benefit
At Issue		
1	$0	$746,050
2	$34,318	$755,884
3	$35,527	$714,076
4	$35,527	$671,368
5	$35,527	$628,368
6	$35,527	$627,782
7	$35,527	$615,993
8	$35,527	$598,993
9	$35,527	$599,520
10	$35,527	$574,204
11	$35,527	$531,479
12	$35,527	$517,900
13	$35,527	$500,829
14	$35,527	$459,076
15	$35,527	$438,087
16	$35,527	$427,775
17	$35,527	$404,654
18	$35,527	$361,946
19	$35,527	$336,060
20	$35,527	**$324,300**
Total	**$673,804**	

There is still a legacy of **$324,300** even after taking an income of **$673,804** over the duration of his retirement!

Researchers like Roger Ibbotson point to the right kinds of annuities as a better income source for many retirees than bonds, the traditional fixed-income investment. (Ibbotson is also the creator of a chart known as the SBBI [Stocks, Bonds, Bills, and Inflation] chart, famous in investment circles, that shows that stocks have far outperformed bonds in terms of investment return since 1945.) Think of it—the guy who invented the "Stocks Beats Bonds" chart is now a fan of annuities. Unheard of.

I am a big fan of low-fee or no-fee annuities as a replacement for bonds in at least part of your portfolio. An annuity is a tool, just like stocks or bonds. Annuities can be a very useful tool for people with, let's say, $200,000 to $10 million to invest. By putting half of your nest egg into an annuity with an income rider instead of bonds, you can guarantee a nice income stream based on the claims and paying ability of the underlying insurance company without worrying about the price or stability or marketability of a bond, or the gyrations in the stock market.

ANNUITY LADDER

For Alan and Ashley, needing a relatively modest but steady income stream, I recommended a ladder of fixed-indexed annuities totaling $600,000 that would guarantee them a yield of about 5 percent a year based on the income rider we added for an additional fee (some products even don't charge for their income riders). In addition, Alan took out a reverse mortgage on his house, which pays him a steady income instead of him paying a monthly mortgage, and he bought a guaranteed universal life insurance policy with a face value of $300,000 that will take care of any debt after he dies. The annuity and reverse mortgage provide the income; the life insurance insures a legacy, including long-term care if needed, and would pay off any remaining debt. At the end of the game, they'll have points on the board.

This strategy also makes sense under current tax laws (which admittedly have changed and could change again). If Alan had just kept all his money in a traditional IRA, he'd owe roughly 30 percent to the government in taxes whenever he withdrew cash. Under this strategy, the tax rate is reduced perfectly legally to about 12 percent federal income tax. Worth doing!

It's also a great strategy for times of volatility in markets and politics. The annuities and reverse mortgage take them out of the huge swings of the markets, which are often driven by political risk.

Who needs that? Why not lower your risk and enjoy life?

Less risk and lower fees.

OPTIONALITY

But above all, what I gave Alan and Ashley was what I call "optionality."

Their neighbors, who are still going to all those investment seminars and checking CNBC minute by minute, panic with every big drop on the Dow Jones index, which in the era of electronic and automated trading can happen out of the blue at any time. Alan is serene, because things he had never considered, such as life insurance, a reverse mortgage, and an annuity, have given him certainty. He can stay put or sell the house (and pay back the reverse mortgage), whatever he wants. He's not going to lose his money if the Dow tanks one day.

But it's important to note that everyone's financial situation, desires, obsessions, and tolerance for risk are unique. Given all that I managed to learn about Alan, his past history with investment managers, and how he wanted to live his life, annuities as part of an overall package made a lot of sense.

Sometime in the future we might also have available to us innovative government-backed infrastructure bonds called, cleverly, SeLFIES, for Standard of Living indexed, Forward-starting, Income-only Securities. They don't exist yet, but they would be bonds issued by the Treasury, available to all, that you'd buy during your earning years, and which pay out for 20 years after you retire, an amount that's indexed both to inflation and to the standard of living as measured by various government indexes. By gradually accumulating the government-guaranteed bonds, you can target, say, a $50,000 annual income for the 20 years between ages 65 and 85. In some states, like New Jersey, it's called Secure Choice.[2]

Stay tuned.

ACTION STEPS

- Learn about the four types of annuities and match yourself with one of the objectives.
- Consider well-structured and appropriate annuities that will provide a steady stream of income while lowering risk.
- Favor annuities that can be adjusted if market conditions change, but that still charge relatively low fees.
- Use excess income from the annuities to add security by buying life insurance that will provide long-term care, pay off debts for the estate, and offer a legacy to heirs.
- New and improved annuities have low costs, too, and leave money to your heirs when you die.
- I want to be clear here: annuities have their cons. Namely, you don't buy an annuity for growth, you buy an annuity for income. Some have surrender charges, although now you can buy ones that have *zero* surrender charges. Some have high fees, while others have *zero* internal fees. You always want to ask your advisor to show you the low-fee annuities, not just the high-fee ones. Ask them what internal fees and exit fees are. Ask them how long the annuity must be kept in force. Ask them about caps, spreads, and participation rates. The fine print matters.

5

REALITY CHECK

MONTE CARLO IS FOR GAMBLING, NOT WISE MONEY MANAGEMENT. AN EASY-TO-UNDERSTAND GAME PLAN WILL ORGANIZE YOUR FINANCES.

MEET JASON

Jason is a 30-year-old software engineer living in the Cleveland suburb of Shaker Heights. He's married to his wife, Audrey, and they have two small daughters, Becky and Angela. He plays bass in a blues band at dive bars in Cleveland Heights. His Ford F-150 with 185,000 miles and balding tires sits in the garage, and he holds about $150,000 in bank certificates of deposit.

What he didn't have was any idea of when, if, or how he'd be able to stop working in 10 or 15 years and still support his family and lifestyle.

"Is the $150,000 gonna be enough? I gotta get the kids through college. What if somebody gets sick? How long do I have to work?"

These were all the right questions; before we could even begin to answer them for Jason, we needed to set a baseline against which we could play out various options for him. His brain seemed to have what Bob Castiglione calls a "Financial Junk Drawer" mentality. Not that he was disorganized, but he had no framework to evaluate the endless opinions he would hear every day when he turned on the financial talking heads.

When Jason came to us, we sat down and ran all his relevant numbers through a computer program that showed how much money he was likely to have at age 65, 70, 80, and on. Being in software, Jason loved the idea of the program, and we spent an enjoyable couple of hours answering his questions and substituting all kinds of numbers and scenarios.

The bottom line we came up with: with Jason's present income, savings, and prospects, he wasn't going to be able to put two kids through college, keep the F-150 in good shape, and keep the house into retirement without making some key decisions now.

MEET THE ULTIMATE FINANCIAL GAME PLAN FOR RETIREMENT

The software program we ran for Jason was the Ultimate Financial Game Plan for retirement, the tool that all our financial advisors use to assess and prescribe investment plans, but which few people even know about.

Now that you've done an assessment of where you are and where you want to go, it's time to consider what should be a basic tool of all sophisticated financial planners. The point of this brief chapter isn't to provide the details and computer algorithms that our planners use to develop your financial plan. Rather, the point is to get you to realize that it's important to find an advisor who has a solid Financial Game Plan that takes all your information into account and doesn't necessarily try to predict the future (that never works).

A solid plan takes into account all your assets and circumstances and makes sure you or your heirs will be protected against both likely and less-likely problems that may arise. These include, most obviously, a financial recession and stock-market crash, but also unexpected illness, sudden death, disability, job loss, and inflation, and they even include less-heralded factors such as planned obsolescence; in other words, it's why you need to replace your refrigerator every few years. The term "planned obsolescence" means "the business practice of deliberately outdating an item by stopping its supply or service support and introducing a newer often-incompatible model or version." Think of how Apple continually changes its power cords every few years. USB-A begat Lightning cord begat USB-C.

You need The Ultimate Financial Game Plan because, in any game, you need to work on your plays before you play the game. Professional football players, most of whom have played the game for many years, still need to practice their plays before the season and in between each game. They go through simulations of plays and watch hours of film showing their movements and those of their opponents in different situations.

That's just how our Game Plan works. It is a flight simulator for your money. You look at each component—say, exchange-traded funds, stocks, life insurance, or a bond fund—individually, and then the computer tells you how that product and all the other factors work together in a coordinated, integrated fashion.

When was the last time your financial advisor, your tax advisor, your mortgage provider, your private banker, your accountant, and your property and casualty insurance agent all met around a table, discussing what was best for you? We call that the Financial Quarterback Process. I have asked this question in almost 10,000 client interviews, and the answer is always, "I've never had that happen, Josh. I don't know how that would work. Can you show me more?" And that's the beauty of having The Ultimate Financial Game Plan for retirement.

The Game Plan gives you a unified view of your entire life. By adjusting the various components, you and your team of advisors can design a plan that will offer you financial security. Imagine the joy and comfort of knowing that if anything ever happens to you, your spouse or significant other will be okay. If your advisor says she doesn't use a Game Plan, you may want to find another advisor.

MONTE CARLO:
THE CASINO OF MODELS

One of the most popular models is the Monte Carlo Simulation, named after a small principality in the south of France that's best known for Grace Kelly and for its casinos. The basic premise of Monte Carlo is significantly flawed. It takes various financial factors and spits out the probability of how likely you are to run out of money when you're 95, for example. It doesn't do anything in terms of seeing how various financial products fit together in a holistic fashion.

Imagine an airplane pilot going on the loudspeaker before takeoff and telling you there was a 60 percent chance of running out of fuel before you reached your destination. You'd get off that plane as fast as you could. But many people's Monte Carlo simulations give them a 60 percent or 70 percent chance of running out of money while they're still alive and kicking.

My problem with Monte Carlo is that people don't truly understand that the inputs matter. In other words, as a general way of surveying the range of probable retirement shortfalls, it doesn't consider, or doesn't verify, such assumptions as rates of return, inflation, or when you might need the money. That's usually because too few variables are considered.

Think of the average retirement calculator on a major fund-company's website. These usually represent a decent enough starting point, but still nowhere near acceptable for planning a 20- to 40-year-long retirement. Among the major issues are how they look at bond returns: Do they use a historical average, around 3 percent, or do they use the returns from 2008 to 2018 when government bond yields were near zero? Many of these retirement scenarios don't account for that. Our model does. Make sure your model tests your retirement scenario in low-yield bond environments and in high-yield—not just historical—bond averages.

The most important aspect of The Game Plan is game theory. A good model doesn't just use a 30-year historical average, it theorizes best- and worst-case scenarios—for example, zero bond rates, or the benchmark 10-year Treasury Note at 3 percent or less for as far as the eye can see. The same goes for the stock market. Models should paint scenarios ranging everywhere from a crash to the Dow reaching 38,000.

Too few financial model calculators have settings for all the wealth-eroding factors. Our model factors in all these risks. If yours doesn't, get a new model—*now!* Your financial future depends on it.

Does your model account for:

a.   Market risk—high (1980–1990s) and low (2000–2010)
b.   Inflation rates—0 to the stagflation of the 1970s
c.   Planned obsolescence
d.   Technology changing
e.   Fees
f.   Taxes
g.   Lawyers' fees
h.   Increased spending in retirement—many retirement calculators assume we need 70 percent of our pre-retired income to be "okay." I would never use such a general rule of thumb. Everyone has a unique budget. So, what will you spend your money on in retirement? Some spend more money than others. Some spend a lot more. Think of this: On what day of the week do you spend the most money? If you're anything like me, you will probably say the weekend. Isn't retirement supposed to be more like a life of eternal weekends? What do you do on a weekend? What kinds of things do you spend your money on? Dinners out, trips to the Caribbean? Flesh out the list.

A Game Plan should be actionable. To show you some action items considered, I am including results from our Game Plan:

Not Enough Disability Insurance

Consider getting a total of 67 percent of income in disability insurance. For example, if you make $10,000 a month, consider a policy with a monthly benefit of $6,700. Make sure your policy has its own occupation definition of disability. Get a guaranteed, non-cancellable policy. Contact a disability insurance specialist by calling 888-988-5674.

Long-Term Care May Be Needed for Asset Protection

You don't have long-term-care benefits in the event of injury or illness that provides you from preforming activities of daily living (ADLs). With your Leap Professional, consult your health insurance agent for options regarding estate protection.

Will Needs Updating

Have you updated your will to include changes in your life situation? Do you have separate trustees and guardians? Your will was done many years ago, so consider updating your will. It also looks like you don't have a Living Will and Durable Power of Attorney. This is not meant to be a replacement for legal advice.

Get a Revocable Living Trust with Dynastic Provisions

See an estate planning attorney to make sure you maintain your privacy by avoiding the probate process through the use of a living trust. Add dynastic provisions to make sure you creditor-proof and divorce-proof your heirs.

Taking Too Much Risk

You seem to be at a risk of a significant drawdown (as much as 50 percent) if the stock market experiences a significant decline. Consider a risk-tolerance and risk-capacity questionnaire. Consider increasing exposure to fixed income and treasuries.

THE GAME PLAN

I say get off that model and try something different. I prefer my proprietary model, The Financial Quarterback Game Plan™.

I like my model because—sticking with the football analogy I used earlier—it puts all the financial players—offense and defense—on the field and working in symphony. In our program, we analyze the destroyers of your offense as well. We analyze the opposing team, we stock up on our players, and we make sure you have a great offense and a good defense.

The Game Plan has three components:

1. It's based on the principle of the protection theory of money. We want to protect your life, your income, and your health first. Think of the offensive line. You want to make sure your quarterback does not get sacked.
2. Our tool is different than anything else, because it is holistic: you can see every player in your financial life organized in a framework, much like a play in a football game.
3. It's fun. It's like fantasy football for your money. You can play and run the movie of your life. You can see what would happen if your quarterback got sacked, but you will also be aware of various things that may hurt you if you do not look at your life in a coordinated and integrated fashion.

You'd never play a football game without a game plan. You couldn't do it. A coach needs to call the play. They watch the films repeatedly to see how they're going to prepare. That's the same thing with our financial Game Plan. We watch the movies, we run the film, and you win the game.

To be clear, the Game Plan is not a predictive tool. It's based on the principle that we cannot predict the future. Black-swan events will occur, and interest rates may rise. You put a scenario in the model where you ask, "What happens if bond interest rates go up?" You play that movie, and you look at something else, and you say, "Well, what happens if bond interest rates go down?" And then you run that movie.

Bonds and stocks may not be your only worry, so we allow for role playing various scenarios. For example, the early demise of your spouse, a disability, or a long-term-care illness. One of the unique things about the Game Plan is that it shows health-care costs in retirement, which could have an inflation rate of 12 percent compared to long-term-care costs, which may have an inflation rate of 3 to 6 percent. The beauty of the Game Plan is you can simultaneously see your many risks at once. It's based on game theory, not Monte Carlo.

DE-FENSE WINS!

In the year 2001, the Baltimore Ravens won the Super Bowl, thanks to their defensive prowess. Their offense was mediocre, but their defense won the championship. Some teams don't have a great offense but make it to the Super Bowl because their defense sticks. In general, it's defense that wins championships. In 2018, the Patriots and Eagles both had good offenses. Tom Brady had the most passing yards in any Super Bowl game ever and the Patriots still lost. The Eagles had the better defense. Defense is the critical component to a financial plan as well. All of the offense won't do any good if your quarterback gets sacked due to the big three opposing forces (disability, death, or unemployment).

The other component that is critical to any football team or fantasy football game is player management, equivalent to cash flow in a financial plan. Our cash-flow tool makes sure you have enough money to field a team that will win the game. The cash-flow tool incorporates your income to buy the various players and uses debt to increase your cash flow so that you may buy better players, train existing players, and improve their skills.

First, we'll identify the defensive players (see page 98). In the 3-4-4 formation, you have three defensive linemen, four linebackers, and four defensive backs—two safeties and two cornerbacks. Your first three are your initial line of defense. These are your car insurance, home or renter's insurance, and umbrella—otherwise known as excess liability insurance. These are your first line of defense if you have a car accident, damage to your dwelling pace, or excess liability or lawsuits.

Next, we'll visit your linebackers. These positions help you "sack" the opposing forces of long-term disability, illness, or other medical issues. That includes disability insurance, long-term-care insurance, medical, dental, and vision insurance, and Social Security insurance—which we'll pay special attention to now. Disability is important because you need two-thirds of your income in the form of disability insurance. Why not take 1 percent of your paycheck and ensure the other 99 percent? Why do we say get a disability policy equal to 67 percent of your predisability earnings? Because if you buy a policy with after-tax dollars, the benefit is tax-free, assuming the government—both federal and state income tax—erodes about 33 percent of your earnings: that's why we say two-thirds. You could always work a little longer if you're not disabled. But if you're disabled and work paycheck to paycheck, a disability could wipe you out. Long-term-care insurance is something that people think is too costly, but many people are spending upwards of $10K or more per month on end-of-life care. Your kids may love you but not be able to care for you in your older age. A properly designed long-term-care insurance package can help protect you from the dreaded Medicaid spend-down.

The final four defensive backs are meant to intercept the ball of the opposing forces. What can oppose you? Well, just as a Hail Mary pass may hit the end zone, the job of the D-backs is to defend against far-off-in-our-mind threats like death through wills and trusts, how your business is structured, term life insurance if you have an early demise (do you have an income to replace the bread-winner or nanny to replace the parent who may work at home?), and trusts to divorce-proof and creditor-proof the heirs and make sure the money is going where you direct it—minimizing state taxes through certain irrevocable trusts.

Now let's identify the offensive players (see page 99). Any good offense must have a strong O-line. Social Security, government bonds, cash-value life insurance, cash equivalents, and municipal bonds bring a protection element to your offense, as the focus is on conservative money for emergencies and income. Their job is to protect the quarterback against opposing forces by focusing on protection of income and assets. The Financial Quarterback™ process comes in to help you align and coordinate your players, since you are the owner of your team. The quarterback may call the plays, but you own the team. You have three total receivers on the team. Your wide receivers have one objective—to catch the long ball. Your three wide receivers are your stocks (by stocks, we also mean equities, exchange-traded funds, and mutual funds), your business interests, and alternate investments like gold, silver, hedge funds, or cryptocurrencies. Just as an offense cannot solely rely on the deep threat, so must your financial offense have more current slow-growth assets, represented by the running back of bonds or annuity income. They may not catch a 30-yard pass, but they can run for 5 yards. It's essential to have more conservative assets to weather uncertainty in the market.

So, think of 11 players on offense, 11 players on defense, and a cash-flow analysis to make sure you have the right budget to win the game.

And in case you think this game stuff is silly, I'm convinced that gaming will be the future of financial literacy in America. Many kids grow up knowing how to create fantasy worlds and zap bad guys on their Xboxes, but without a game plan for their money. This game analogy could be the way to educate an entire generation in matters of financial literacy.

Our Game Plan makes sure that everything you have right now is protected, that if uncertainties come—and we know they will—you are prepared. How would your plan fare in the event of a disability, a lawsuit, or a sudden market drop? Are you not only ready for bad news, but ready to take advantage of it?

Are you 100 percent certain you're prepared for what catastrophies life may bring? Clients who go through the Game Plan are prepared.

A lot of advisors, especially with big firms, say they can predict a crash with accuracy, and they'll help you get out of it. I did happen to see the 2007–2008 crash coming and warned my clients. But I also remember some serious people saying that their models were showing that the market would crater in early 2016. One book prophesied financial destruction due to the Shemitah, a biblical reference. To be sure, the markets are often uncertain and current events may be scary at times. But soon thereafter, the market went up like a rocket. This reinforced my view that the answer to financial uncertainty is not a prediction, but a modeling tool that has the appropriate amounts dedicated toward protection, utilizing a model that allows you to stay in the market. *You have the most success when you don't let fear drive your decisions.*

The only certainty we have is the present. There is so much beyond your control. We never know what the current stock market is doing. We don't know what future tax rates or interest rates will be. When an advisor enters data representing your present financial situation, our model helps us understand what you're doing right and where you might improve. It's programmed to reveal ideas that might make things lower volatility and more conservative. The idea is to identify your ideal financial position, given your specific circumstances.

From there, we start a process that helps you create the ideal financial plan, which we ask you to update every year, or more often if you lose your job, get married, have another kid, or win the lottery. Any significant life change should be accompanied by a new look at your Game Plan. Run the play and see if you can win the game.

In contrast to reading boring graphs and charts, the Financial Quarterback Game Plan visually shows you how you're doing. When you see your Game Plan, you may identify issues like:

I don't have enough protection.

I'm paying too much on premiums.

I don't have enough savings.

I have too much invested in growth stocks that could tumble if the market falls.

I have too much in tax-deferred or tax-deductible accounts.

JASON'S LINEUP

Jason from Shaker Heights, a long-suffering Cleveland Browns fan, got the football analogy right away.

He already had health and disability insurance from his company, as well as auto and homeowner's insurance. Since he is a healthy nonsmoker, we got him a life insurance policy at reasonable rates, which is going to protect him now and provide income in the form of tax-free withdrawals later when he needs it. The death benefit on the policy could also help in the event Jason needs long-term care.

With his defense set, we went on offense. As those CDs matured, we invested in stock and bond ETFs in about a 50/50 ratio. He had never bothered with a 401(k), even though his employer offered one, so we got him to take advantage of his employer match. He found $500 a month through our cash flow budget tool that he could put away in a savings account.

That was a lot of change for Jason; but given that he could look at and fiddle with the model himself, it all made sense.

He felt secure and confident.

He put new tires on the F-150.

GAME PLAN RECAP

The Game Plan considers more than two dozen possible investment vehicles, including stocks, bonds, ETFs, and tax-deferred annuities and tax-free bonds, as well as types of protection ranging from car insurance to health insurance to disability insurance to property insurance to liability coverage to whole life to long-term-care insurance. It also considers areas of growth and tax savings. Then it looks at how these various items do or do not work together—do your investments and insurance choices maximize tax savings, for example? Lack of coordination can mean you're paying more fees or taxes than you need to, or not generating as much income as you could. Most importantly: it's fun!

The Financial Quarterback Game Plan follows. The first 11 of these points are the defensive line that everyone needs to feel secure. The second 11 are your offense. In the same way that every good football team has 300-pound men who protect the quarterback, the following measures may protect you:

THE FINANCIAL QUARTERBACK GAME PLAN

DEFENSIVE LINE

1. **Car Insurance**
   a. Do you have it?
   b. What's your premium?
   c. What are your deductibles?
   d. Are you paying for deductibles that don't benefit you? Meaning, if you scratched your bumper and had a deductible of $500, would you submit the claim?
   e. Do you have the maximum protection in the event of an accident?
   f. What are your liability limits?
   g. Does your coverage go down if you hit someone who is underinsured or has no insurance? Studies have shown that 13 percent of accidents are with people who have no insurance.
   h. Consider getting an attorney to draft a release for small fender-benders so your premiums don't go up.
   i. Remember to submit big claims but avoid little ones.

2. **Home Insurance**
   a. Do you have it?
   b. What's your premium?
   c. What are your deductibles?
   d. Are you paying for deductibles you wouldn't use for fear of premiums going up? Meaning, if you lost some jewelry and had a rider on your home insurance that covered jewelry and had a deductible of $500, would you submit the claim?

    e. Do you have the maximum protection in the event of an accident?

    f. What are your liability limits?

    g. Does your coverage offer full replacement value?

    h. Remember to submit big claims but avoid little ones.

3.   **Umbrella Policy**

    a. Do you have it?

    b. What's your premium?

    c. What are your deductibles?

*Your Linebackers = The first 4 in the 3-**4**-4 defense*

    4. Disability Insurance

    5. Long-Term-Care Insurance

    6. Medical, Dental, and Vision Insurance

    7. Social Security Insurance

*Your Defensive Backs = The second 4 in the 3-4-**4** defense*

    8. Life Insurance

    9. Wills

    10. Trusts—including a plan for your beloved Fido

    11. Asset Protection and Ownership arrangements

YOUR OFFENSE

Your Receivers

    1. Stocks

    2. Business

    3. Alternate Investments

Your Offensive Linemen—the five big guys who protect your quarterback
   4. Social Security
   5. Government Bonds
   6. Cash-Value Life Insurance
   7. Municipal Bonds
   8. Cash Equivalents

The Quarterback and Short Offensive Catch and
Run Game
   9. Quarterback: Financial Advisor
  10. Running Back: Annuities
  11. Tight End: Corporate Bonds

THE CASH FLOW OF YOUR TEAM
SALARY CAP (BUDGET) AND DEBT RELIEF

This book is really a deep dive into various aspects of our Financial Quarterback Game Plan, and how and why each product
or investment should be deployed, in many cases told through
the real stories of real people. The Game Plan brings all these
ideas into a coherent whole: it doesn't predict, but rather it
prescribes actions that may guard you against the variety of
WEFs: Wealth-Eroding Factors. These include death, disability,
in-laws, outlaws, creditors, predators, lawsuit protections, fee
erosions, planned wear and tear, spending changes—and more!

ACTION STEPS

- Start your planning by asking your advisor to show you your own personal holistic economic financial Game Plan. If he or she doesn't use a model to verify economic decisions—run from them.
- Don't expect it to predict the future: use it to evaluate the present and make the present more efficient. The Game Plan is a simulative tool, which is meant more to prepare you for the future instead of predicting the unknowable.
- Make sure your Game Plan is tailored to your situation and *not* a cookie-cutter calculator on your 401(k) or 403(b) websites. Go to retirementrealitycheck.com and our website will customize a three-tiered approach and tell you exactly how much you should allocate to each of these three strategies: 1) low risk, 2) moderate risk, and 3) high risk.
- In consultation with your advisor, adjust your investments and insurance coverages accordingly, flagging where you might not be able to follow the advice completely.

PART II

SAVE IT!

6

REALITY CHECK

START SAVING AND
DON'T LET FEAR
DRIVE YOUR INVESTING TRAIN!

MEET BRENDA

Brenda is a childhood friend of mine. Brenda and I reconnected after three decades of intermittent contact and a few Facebook posts. At age 36, she had a great job as a sales representative for a major tech company, was earning about $180,000 a year, and saving a third of it. But she was keeping it all in cash, earning about zero interest.

She had called and asked to see me because she wanted the $200,000 she had managed to save to grow beyond the miniscule returns she was getting from the bank.

We caught up and talked about her dreams. It turns out that Brenda is a typical millennial who wants to retire in her 50s and enjoy life but fears the stock market.

In a sense, millennials have jumped a generation and mirror the fears of their grandparents, who survived the Great Depression and, with some justification, didn't think Wall Street could be trusted with their money. Their parents, the baby boomers, were able to capitalize on the booming postwar economy, but recent market downturns and the 2008 crash scared off an entire generation. But the millennials' fears led them to miss one of the biggest stock market booms—2001–2007 and 2009–present—that we've ever seen.

These fears, and a regrettable lack of sophisticated financial knowledge, also led many millennials to spend money stupidly. I think a lot of this goes back to FOMO, a fear of missing out, on experiences or possessions, coupled with a desire not to make the same investing mistakes their parents might have made.

LAZY CASH

Typically, millennials like Brenda might have lots of cash that isn't doing anything for them. Retirement is for their parents or grand-parents, and often brings up images of retirement communities or nursing homes. The stock market is scary, and if they do buy some stocks, they sell when the market goes down, dooming any hopes of getting that money back.

Some fail to take advantage of the miracle of the exponential curve.

Once it's explained to them, I find that millennials can intui-tively grasp this, but fear of things going wrong makes them keep everything in cash. They're the most cash-oriented generation since the greatest generation. They distrust the market. And although dismissed as "snowflakes," they are surprisingly responsible with their money. Maybe due to hoarding so much money while living with their parents, or precisely by doing the opposite of what their parents did—saving. "Sha la la la la la live for today" has become "Save it for a rainy day."

They also understand that protection matters. Will I be okay financially if I become disabled, if my spouse dies or is disabled, or if there's a crisis? Why don't you plan for that? People say, "Well, I can't plan for that." But millennials do want a plan for that.

Yes, you can. You *can* plan for the unknowns. It's called buying insurance! You *can* have a cash buffer and you *can* get guaranteed streams of income. If you have disability insurance, life insurance, and guaranteed-income insurance, you're protected against what I call "the big three." The three most common risks to a financial plan are: death, disability, and loss of income through unemployment or retirement. Then you can let the rest of your money rip in low-cost strategies designed for higher growth potential. Essentially, you could then be more aggressive with the rest and take a long-term position in the stock market, because you've taken care of the biggest risk that you have: the risk of doing something stupid.

MEET LARRY, CURLY, AND MOE

People tend to let fear get the best of them. Take the case of three friends in their 50s, whom we'll call Larry, Curly, and Moe.

They're all small-business owners and they've all made about the same salary since they started working fresh out of college, 30 years ago. They go out for drinks after work together and catch a ball game at Madison Square Garden whenever they can. They all despair of ever seeing the Knicks win another championship. At least the Knicks have a better chance than the Detroit Lions (my team). But that's where the similarities end.

Larry has managed to accumulate $6 million.

Curly has $2 million to his name.

Moe has a relatively paltry $200,000 (no shame).

What happened?

Larry stayed in the market through all its ups and downs, periodically adjusting his holdings but sticking with small capitalization stocks, with a dash of FAANG (Facebook, Apple, Amazon, Netflix, Google) because he uses all those products and pays attention to social media. His principle is simple—never sell, and save 20 percent of his income.

Curly sold a bit late in 2008, but later stuck with his convictions and didn't put too much back into the market. He missed a fair amount of upside the last decade. He was a good saver but didn't have the stomach for the market.

Moe bought and sold at completely the wrong times, loading up in 2007 at the height of the market, selling in 2008, and then got married and bought a nice car, a nice house, and a nice boat, instead of putting money back in the market. He had fun, but he's got a long life ahead of him with worries about paying for it.

Larry never let fear get the best of him.

Curly let the market fool him. Had he set up a volatility buffer, he might have more money now.

Moe spent a lot. And another note: all three are married, but Curly's and Larry's wives were in on the process and agreed to save at least 10 percent of their income.

Moe's wife neglected planning. Moral of the story: *bring your honey into the money decisions.* Or vice versa. I have seen many couples fail at planning because of disagreements. I get it. I try to avoid money fights with my darling wife of many years if possible. But proper financial planning is a great act of love.

So, how do you start saving and get out of debt to start your retirement reality check?

CHUNKING

One strategy we use for getting out of debt on the start of your savings journey is what I call "chunking."

If you get a $500 gift or a $5,000 bonus check, throw it all against your highest credit-card balance. Resist the urge to blow it on things that will land in a garage sale a few years from now. That will take a big chunk out of your total debt. It will give you a great sense of satisfaction to keep going.

If you've got credit-card debt, try to pay it off in chunks; throw all of that $1,000 bonus or $2,500 from a part-time project against the credit-card balance until it's gone. Once you've got some savings, the trick is to make them work hard for you and increase your income. Few do this now—and everybody should.

THE ENVELOPE TECHNIQUE

Let's look for a minute at one popular savings strategy, the so-called "envelope technique," used, or at least tried, by an astonishing number of people.

The envelope technique was introduced to me by longtime friends and clients Cindy and Bill. It was pioneered by Larry Burkett, who was the Dave Ramsey before Dave Ramsey, and one of the first Christian-oriented investment advisors. He seemed a well-intentioned guy, but if a strategy is judged by its fruit, it may be deemed ineffective. The general populace seems no better off.

Here's the envelope technique:

Say you have net earnings of $5,000 a month. You would take that and literally or electronically put all of it in various "envelopes." Rent. Car payment. Credit-card payment. You're allowed to carry over money from one envelope to the same envelope next month, but you can't move money between envelopes in any given month. For example, once your food envelope hits zero, you are only to eat what's in your cupboard. Once your credit-card envelope hits zero, you can't make any more charges on your credit cards.

Now, here's the thing: it is a great method *if you follow it*. It works. If somebody making $30,000 to $50,000 a year actually abides by the rules, it is one of the best techniques to get your budget under control. It will eventually get you out of debt if you don't use a credit card. Just take your money, put it in an envelope, and pay all your bills. But very few people are actually able to stick with this technique!

Then along came Dave Ramsey and Suze Orman, who basically took Larry Burkett and popularized him for today. They preach (I'm simplifying) forgoing that Starbucks latte or that Netflix subscription until you've paid off your credit-card debt. It may be small stuff, but it's still deprivation with little enjoyment, and the average person may give up on the technique.

We'll go into the right approach for today. It works better in that it's easy and it works under the presumption that most people cut or increase their standard of living based on what's in their bank account. So, we still have you live paycheck to paycheck. You just don't see where the other money is going until you've accumulated a significant amount.

AUTOSAVE: A BETTER ENVELOPE STRATEGY

Go to human resources (HR) and ask for four autosave direct deposits. Autosave 1: your normal checking account for day-to-day expenses. No more than 70 percent of your salary should go to a checking account, from which you'll pay living expenses. Autosave 2: your workplace retirement plan. Make sure you save at least 10 percent in your Roth 401(k) or traditional 401(k) or other workplace retirement plan. Autosave 3: the third is 10 percent to a long-term savings cash account. This could be a high-yield money market, a cash-value life insurance policy with a high early cash amount, or a savings account. The key here is it's not tied to your checking. With this simple approach, you've got enough to live on and you're still saving 20 percent of your net income—and if you do that, odds are you'll become a financial success. Autosave 4: if so inclined, give the other 10 percent to your favorite shul, church, or charity. What is the key to life? Is it the most stuff or the most blessings we can give to others?

What all my clients and potential clients have in common is that they've never stopped to analyze their financial situations in a holistic approach. This approach puts money away conservatively while generating income, opens up a bunch of other income streams from assets that they already have, turns the tax code into an opportunity rather than a burden, establishes a spending strategy that lets them enjoy life, and provides for a legacy. I think the autosave is most important because it tethers you to what really matters.

ACTION STEPS

- Identify your *real* investment risk tolerance by using the powerful Risk Assessment on our website.
- Pick an advisor or talk to your current advisor about issues such as increasing revenue streams, establishing a volatility buffer, optimizing tax strategies, and establishing an insurance plan.
- Create a plan to diversify out of cash, if cash is all you have.
- When you're working with someone, pick a plan before you pick a product.
- If you've got credit-card debt, pay it off in chunks.

7

REALITY CHECK

DON'T LOSE MONEY IN THE NEXT STOCK MARKET CRASH. CREATE A VOLATILITY BUFFER.

BRENDA CALLS

In second grade, I had been the only boy invited to my friend Brenda's Cabbage Patch party. Oddly enough, I had a Cabbage Patch doll when I was young. Cabbage Patch dolls all feature characteristic chubby cheeks and hundreds of varieties of hairstyles and attire, and each had its own unique name. Mine was named Meyer Dickie.

When Brenda met me in my office years later, we started to reminisce. Eventually she cut back to the present: "What do I do, Josh? My family—like yours—never had much money. You're successful. Where do I put my money?"

After Brenda came to me, we immediately started making maximum allowable contributions to her 401(k) retirement plan (something millennials tend to ignore). We didn't put much in the stock market because at the time there was a real possibility of a downturn from record highs.

We then set up her volatility buffer, consisting of putting $25,000 a year into a dividend-paying participating permanent cash-value life insurance policy and $25,000 a year into a portfolio of small-cap stock funds. At age 55, she'll have put in $725,000 and have $2.8 million to retire on. If she doesn't touch this money until age 75, she'll have more than $6 million.

There are, of course, pitfalls Brenda needs to avoid. Let's say she wants to pay for her kids' college when that time comes. Traditional planning would have her sell the stocks and pay the tuition. A couple of four-year college careers funded this way would shrink her age-55 nest egg 10 years prior to retirement.

Instead, assuming Brenda keeps listening to me, she'll borrow what she needs for the college expenses from her whole-life policy, paying herself back gradually, and with interest. She won't lose much compounding, if any, and she gets to see her nest egg keep growing. One of the unique benefits of a nondirect recognition life-insurance policy is that it credits you the same dividend even if you borrowed a significant amount of money from your policy. That lets you use your money and still have it growing for you as though you never touched it.[1]

Another advantage, and indeed the key advantage, of a volatility buffer, which could be a whole-life policy or an annuity or a bond ladder, is that it carries a minimum rate of return. The stock market might beat this return on the way up, but it may hurt a lot on the way down. Making a conservative 4 percent a year (compounded) allows Brenda to stick with the volatility of the market in order to achieve the market-like returns over a 20-year period. The volatility buffer will help her—and you—not vomit out your portfolio when the stock market becomes a roller coaster.

Brenda's still working, but she's sleeping a lot better at night knowing that, for the first time in her life, she's making more than zero interest on her savings. She's on track, protected, and isn't going to freak out if the stock market goes down. She's never watched CNBC and isn't about to start.

LIFE'S TRADE-OFFS

Life is a series of trade-offs, and sometimes even at a relatively early age trading a possible higher return from risky investments for the security and optionality of a volatility buffer makes a lot of sense. I have found over the years that giving this technique a name—a volatility buffer—rather than just saying "put some money away in safe investments and life insurance"—is much more powerful and constantly reminds the client what's going on. This is their buffer against unexpected expenses or bad times. Buffers are good and sound a lot safer than "bank account."

For my millennial clients, with plenty of time left before they retire, I recommend a blended strategy: 50–80 percent in an aggressive portfolio of stocks, no-load mutual funds, and ETFs; 20–50 percent in conservative investments including cash-value life insurance that will grow at 4 percent a year or higher, tax-free and compounded. One benefit of this is that it precludes the need for a term life insurance policy purchase.

Another is that it takes advantage of compound interest, which Albert Einstein is rumored to have called the "most powerful force in the Universe." Compound interest gets its power from being exponential. The amount you earn interest on grows every year. Whether Einstein said it or not, getting your investments on the exponential curve is a great strategy. In general, on this curve your original investment doubles every 10 years at a hypothetical 7 percent rate of return.

The volatility buffer is probably the one thing in anybody's life that grows exponentially. It's part of a strategy that also includes market investments, and a spend-down strategy (we'll talk about this later); and, if properly structured, it means you'll never have to sell those equities during a crisis or market downturn. A volatility buffer is a store of money that grows and provides a source of cash when it's needed. The type of buffer I usually recommend is a cash-value life insurance properly constructed from a reputable life insurance company. These policies pay dividends or earn index credits. I call these SWAN (sleep well at night) policies.

While it can get a bit technical, the point is that this volatility buffer brings with it what I like to call "optionality."

Let's say the market crashes, and maybe you lose your job and need some cash. Instead of selling your stocks at their now-depressed prices, you can take a loan against the money you have in the whole-life policy and pay the loan back, with the interest going to yourself! When the market goes back up, you can sell some shares and repay the loan. It works like the hedges that billionaires use. It gives you options and may let you keep your stocks. The best portfolio is one you don't have to liquidate when the market falls.

The whole idea of a volatility buffer is that it's money you can draw from if you really need it if there's a crash, so that you don't touch your equity.

MEET MARY, DARA, HAROLD, AND JOHN

Mary is a 58-year-old doctor who wants to retire at 65. She has saved $2.5 million for retirement and feels good about it. She knows exactly what she wants to do: grow that $2.5 million to $3 million in seven years in order to retire and live off that money, invested half in stocks and half in annuities—50 percent in equities, 50 percent annuities.

That will be a great place to be, but how does she get there?

She needs to set up a volatility buffer right now.

It would be best for Mary to use an annuity as her buffer. An annuity is just a savings account with an insurance company. They're promising you a stream of payments backed by their underlying creditworthiness.

Your advisor can help you find a good, solid insurance company that's highly rated, but also has assets, measured by capital and surplus cash, that's equal to about 105 percent of their liabilities. That's a safe cushion. Even if the company goes under, they will have treasuries and assets backing every dollar of liability. Your advisor can also help you pick the right kind of annuity. We'll go into this more in the next chapter.

Remember, Mary wants to make $500,000 over seven years. Let's say she puts $1 million in an annuity and puts her other $1.5 million in the market. She'll get a guaranteed $50,000 a year from the annuity, so over seven years she'll make $350,000 of the $500,000 she's looking for. She then needs $150,000 from the $1.5 million in the market. That's 10 percent over seven years—totally doable even if there's a downturn for a while.

Even if there's a real crash and the $1.5 million goes down to $800,000 or even $500,000, she can keep her diversified investments and live off the $50,000 guaranteed from the annuity until the market rebounds.

Mary's colleague Dara is 44. She's known that she should be in the stock market for 20 years, but she's a little scared. For her, the answer would be a volatility buffer consisting of permanent life insurance. It's a fund that grows tax-free and can be pulled out tax-free.

She can invest in what's called an LIRP, a life insurance retirement plan. She'll pay into the policy for a minimum of seven years, or until she's 65. When she retires, she can take tax-free loans that would give her a guaranteed income that she can't outlive. When she dies, the remaining money passes tax-free to her heirs or a favored charity.

Another of Mary and Dara's colleagues, Harold, is 48 and wants to retire at 55. Harold set up a plan to put away $100,000 a year for seven years in a life insurance policy. When he does retire, the annuity will give him an extra $49,000 a year tax-free, which will supplement his equity and bond investments. It's a great volatility buffer, because he won't have all his money in the market but doesn't need to buy bonds that might yield him little or nothing.

Still another doctor, John, is the most conservative of the bunch. He wants to invest in bonds but wants to earn at least a little something. For John, we set up a bond ladder. These were popular before interest rates sat near zero after 2009, but they are coming back into favor as rates rise.

There are several products from a few companies that we could have picked. For example, there are exchange-traded funds (ETFs), which own bonds that mature in 2020, 2021, or 2022. All the components have different rates of return, but if one bond goes under, you're protected because each fund may own a thousand bonds. There are also more conservative funds that only own US Treasuries of different maturities. Even if the bond market goes crazy, the Treasury is backing the underlying bonds.

ACTION STEPS

- Establish a volatility buffer stocked with a cash-value life insurance policy, or an annuity, or a well-structured bond ladder, for a portion of your assets.
- If you never need to touch this money, great. But in a pinch, borrow against the balance to pay expenses, instead of liquidating stocks. You will pay yourself back, with interest, tax-free.
- This buffer can give you financial security and keep your growth assets growing.

8

REALITY CHECK

HOW TO GENERATE 10 CHECKS IN RETIREMENT BY CREATING NEW REVENUE STREAMS.

MEET PATRICK

Patrick, the burly former law enforcement officer we met earlier, fell into misfortune through past advisors who managed to lose him half his savings twice in the last decade.

Understandably, these experiences with two different big-bank investment advisors left him with a bad taste for my profession. It also left him with the impression—reinforced by the Depression-era mindset of his parents—that the stock market is a place to lose money, not to make money.

The problem with both of Patrick's previous advisors is that they, like most advisors, picked their investments by looking at last year's winners. They were late and usually wrong. It's easy to think that the best fund in Morningstar's ratings last year will also be the best next year, but that's rarely the case.

When Patrick came to me with his $500,000 and a paid-up house, he wanted to let me know he wanted something different from an advisor. I took it as a measure of trust and friendship, but also a bit of a warning, when, after a couple of meetings, he took me along with his fiancée, Alice, to shoot rifles at a gun range near his home. I was touched that he wanted to share his hobby with me, but I also took away an unspoken message: "Don't screw with me." (It was great fun. I shot a bull's-eye the first time. Patrick is a good teacher. He certainly got my attention.) I later learned that he had used his law-enforcement experience to do a complete background check on me and came to one meeting with a thick binder containing my entire life. Clean.

Fortunately for us all, I had no intention of screwing him again out of his savings. Instead of putting all his money in last year's best-performing mutual funds, we set up multiple revenue streams for him.

We kept $100,000 in interest-bearing treasuries as a volatility buffer, and $400,000 in annuities. From the annuity payments, we reserved $40,000 to buy a cash-value life insurance policy that will pay his daughter $600,000 when he dies.

Even after buying the life insurance, the annuities gave Patrick plenty to live on. While annuities may not produce as much income as stock funds in an up market, and indeed they aren't expected to, they are conservative and income-oriented. Income is good. Believe me, with Patrick I wasn't going to take any chances!

MEET JEFFREY AND MAUREEN

Maureen is one of the sweetest women I've ever met—four feet, seven inches of compassion and heart. She and her husband, Jeffrey, found each other late in their lives, and they have been devoted to each other ever since.

Both state employees, they managed to put $600,000 away for retirement mainly by living frugally. They might take the occasional inexpensive vacation to the Econo Lodge in Ocean City, New Jersey, during the off-season, when the rates are lower, strolling on the boardwalk, holding hands.

They came to one of my seminars early in my career at the Lobster Shanty restaurant in Toms River, New Jersey, and later they came to one of my early-career offices back in the day when I could only afford a small, one-room office inside the law office of Bill Heiring.

They had been taken advantage of a little bit by a previous advisor, who had them in some high-fee variable annuities with 4 percent fees. They were able to take advantage of a bunch of income streams new to them. I quickly switched them over to no-load funds, established a volatility buffer with a whole-life insurance policy, and put the rest of the money into a no-internal-fee annuity and some safe high-yield moderate dividend-paying stocks.

They've been happy ever since, and Maureen is one of the biggest stars of my annual client Christmas/Hanukkah party, dancing the night away. In fact, she had demanded that I throw a Christmas party as one of the conditions of signing on as a client, as well as getting a Keurig machine in my office, just as her previous advisor had. No problem. Nobody can resist Maureen!

CHECK THIS LIST

There are 10 major ways to create additional revenue streams to supercharge your retirement funds. Ten potential checks each month!

1. Work to maximize your Social Security payouts by delaying Social Security and doing a maximizesocialsecurity.com calculation.
2. Maximize pension benefits, using life insurance as a volatility buffer.
3. Use annuities.
4. Maximize bond income.
5. Use dividends from stocks and REITs.
6. Use income from a tax-free Roth IRA.
7. Plan to spend down assets.
8. Take the required minimum distributions from IRAs and 401(k)s.
9. Use rental income from real estate.
10. Take a tax-free reverse mortgage.

This chapter is about the outcome from all the planning we've talked about previously. Many of my clients are rightly concerned about the yields from their investments, something they can easily measure in the newspaper or online. But fewer are concerned with what really matters—the income they can generate.

People must become income-oriented to furnish a comfortable retirement. The move from obsession with *growth* to obsession with *income* is a little like the difficulty people have when moving from earning dollars by working to having their dollars do the work.

Let's take them one at a time:

1. Social Security is a lifeline for many disabled and elderly people, but it is primarily a long-term insurance plan for which you've paid premiums all your working life. Like any government program, it has complex rules, and its benefits can vary greatly, depending on how much you've paid in over the years

and when you and your spouse elect to start taking the benefits. The right choices at the right time can give you $3,000 or $4,000 a month more of the money you've paid in over the years. It merits a careful strategy to maximize your benefits. You only have one chance to get it right! You can apply as early as age 62, but you'll get a lot more if you wait until age 66 or 70. The benefits are taxable, so I always consider a client's entire financial picture before fitting the Social Security piece into the puzzle. We'll talk more about Social Security in Reality Check Twelve.

2. If you're entitled to a government or corporate pension (as opposed to owning a 401(k) or IRA from past employers), there are ways to channel these funds into annuities or life insurance policies that can serve as a volatility buffer, so you don't have to spend this money on ongoing expenses. As we've seen earlier, life insurance offers enhanced optionality—including the possibility of taking loans for unexpected expenses.

3. As we've seen, annuities are a much-maligned and often-overlooked way of organizing your savings into a safe and steady stream of income. The right type of annuity may be worth considering as part of your plan.

4. While everyone should avoid or break out of bond jail (see the next chapter: it's an overreliance on bonds that just sit as part of a mathematically constructed portfolio), it's a good idea to have a sound mix of high-quality bonds, both taxable and tax-exempt, that provide a conservative, reliable amount of income at maybe 3 percent or 4 percent. This stream isn't necessarily your biggest source of income, but it's great to have. It's likely to be a bigger percentage as you get older.

5. Use dividends from stocks and REITs. A well-structured portfolio should include dividend-paying stocks and perhaps shares in real estate investment trusts that throw off quarterly dividends. This income, though usually taxable, can provide money for daily expenses without touching the principal of the investments.

6. Use income from a tax-free Roth IRA. There are two main flavors of IRAs: the "normal" IRA lets you put in money that grows tax-free until you must withdraw it, at which point you pay income tax on it. With a Roth IRA, you pay tax on the money up front, allowing you to withdraw it tax-free later. This works best if you expect your income to remain high after retirement, which is our goal!

7. Plan to spend down assets. A spend-down plan throws off money for you to spend. The money can come from stock dividends, bond coupons, or annuity payments. If you can match this income closely to monthly spending, your life can be pleasant, and you may have fewer worries. Most people don't realize that if you don't spend down accounts you may leave more to heirs than you really wanted. Don't deprive yourself!

8. Take the required minimum distributions from IRAs and 401(k)s. The IRS requires people who own IRAs or 401(k)s to start making annual withdrawals beginning at age 70½. The exact amounts are determined by a table on the IRS website, and they are taxable (except from a Roth IRA). If you don't take at least the minimum amount, penalties can run as high as 50 percent of the difference between what you take and what you should've taken. It's your money, and taking your required minimum each year gives you money to spend.

9.   Use rental income from real estate. If you've accumulated a spare vacation house or have invested in real estate or downsized to an apartment but kept your house to rent out, these properties could provide reliable monthly income. They also may require maintenance expenses, which can be tax-deductible.

10.   Look into getting tax-free payments via a reverse mortgage. A reverse mortgage, also known as a Home Equity Conversion Mortgage, or HECM, from a reliable provider can offer people age 62 and older monthly cash payments based on their home's value. It's a monthly loan that doesn't get repaid until you sell your house—and use the sale proceeds to pay back the loan. Contrary to popular belief, this is a federally insured loan, and the bank cannot take your home while you are alive. It makes sense for many who own their homes outright and feel cash poor.

Obviously, not everybody is going to be able to take advantage of all 10 of these streams. But most people simply don't think about them and don't exploit these legal and effective ways to increase their monthly incomes in retirement. Using some or all these streams can make the difference between a no-worry retirement and unnecessary stress.

We were able to use about half of the 10 main revenue streams to help Patrick, and a similar number for Jeffrey and Maureen. For other clients, we've used more, depending on the circumstances. It's important to explore them all to make sure you exploit all that apply and are appropriate.

ACTION STEPS

- Use as many of the 10 basic revenue streams as you can to provide income.
- Review the list every couple of years. Some streams that weren't available earlier may now make sense.
- Get your personal customized Social Security Optimizer by going to www.retirement realitycheck.com. Click on the button "Social Security Optimize" to figure out the right claiming strategy for you.

REALITY CHECK

BONDS MAY BE A RECIPE FOR DISASTER. GET OUT OF BOND JAIL. TAKE AIM.

As we saw in Reality Check Four, Alan really loved his bond-like stock, the REIT, which yielded 7 percent but crashed hard after 2008. He saw it as a safe investment that would produce a steady yield at little risk. He was wrong on the specific security—everybody makes mistakes—but more broadly he was wrong on the strategy, which had been preached as gospel for decades—buy and hold dividend-paying stocks.

Another strategy, expounded in countless economics departments and Wall Street sales rooms, involved visualizing an investment pie and dividing it up, sometimes to a stupefying variety of components, among stocks, bonds, and other investments. Get this division right, keep it steady, and eat the pie forever! Another name for the pie is MPT, or Modern Portfolio Theory.

But . . .

The pie is a lie.

The pie is the classic pie chart on every investment statement that shows how many of your assets are in bonds and how many are in stocks and other stuff. A nice, evenly sliced-up pie (half apple, half cherry), or sometimes 60 percent bonds/40 percent stocks, is the ideal.

Wrong.

Putting half or so of your investable assets in bonds and just leaving them there, clipping the coupons and collecting the interest, no matter what, forever, is no longer the best solution for most people, if it ever was. It's really based on a 60-year-old theory from University of Chicago–trained, Nobel Prize–winning economist Harry Markowitz. His research focused on achieving the ideal mix of stocks and bonds in a portfolio based on the level of risk an investor desires, and basically said that fiddling with the portfolio would have little or no effect over time.

As prevalent as this theory has become, it is basically a setup for failure, a 60-year-old idea that needs significant revision.

Many bond funds are as passive as Markowitz ordained: they buy the stuff and keep it. But this ignores the depth and strength and beating heart of the massive bond market—four times as big as the stock market.

Most busy people, even sophisticated investors, don't know that the bond market has been on a 30-year tear, seeming to rise no matter what happens in the economy, through recession, boom, war, and peace. For reasons I have never figured out, it just doesn't get the attention of stocks. You may know whether the Dow Jones Industrial Average (the most popular benchmark for stocks) gained or lost yesterday, but you probably don't know whether the Bank of America Merrill Lynch Global Bond Index gained or lost yesterday!

Stocks are shares in the ownership of a company. They are that company's equity. The same company that issues stock may also borrow money by issuing bonds. Bonds are debt that the company contracts to repay with a certain interest rate, and usually are issued for a fixed period (say, 10 years).

Stocks are valued by how much investors are willing to pay for the stock based on the company's results, market conditions, whatever. Bonds are also traded on exchanges, and their price also depends on how much investors are willing to pay. But unlike with stocks, the interest rate paid on the debt depends on its price. If the price goes up, the rate goes down, and vice versa, sort of like a seesaw. Sadly, you can't get both high interest payments and high prices at the same time; it's one or the other.

Since many investors value the interest paid quarterly or yearly by their bonds or bond funds, and don't want to sell the bonds, a 30-year boom that has kept prices sky-high with yields scraping the bottom of the barrel is actually bad news today! Markowitz's theory may have worked well the last 30 years as bond prices have risen, but what happens when 40–60 percent of your portfolio is falling? And that was the part of the pie not supposed to lose money!

Now, there are price disparities that actively traded funds exploit to increase their value. Smart traders make fortunes by taking calculated risks on distressed and high-yield bonds (often known as junk bonds). These are often issued by government entities or companies that aren't doing very well (often because they already have a lot of debt!). Their prices are very low and they have to offer high yields to get anybody to buy them. But they are also very risky. No FDIC guarantees here; if the company goes bust, you lose. I would never suggest that my clients invest too heavily in junk bonds unless comfortable with the risk, but many traders do make money here. Generally, the passive bond funds marketed as safe for retirees leave a lot of money on the table.

ZERO BOUND

After the 2008 market crash and recession, the Federal Reserve basically cut the interest rate it charges banks—which banks and companies look at to set rates for their bonds—to zero. These near-zero rates led to booming prices for these bonds, but they generated little or no income.

For me, that was already one strike against bonds. Now, that's all changing; and for me and many others, it's strike two.

The Fed has recently ended its low-interest-rate policy, and rates may continue to go up. If you've been following all this, you now know that means bond prices are going down. That could be a recipe for disaster for bond funds, and for the bond market. It's especially problematic because a relatively small interest rate increase can wallop the price of a bond.

Studies by assorted economists and banks have found that for every 1-percent hike in interest rates, the average bond fund's price will go down 8 to 10 percent. Yikes!

NOT SO SAFE

Bonds are not nearly as safe as once thought. If you bought Treasuries in the 1990s when interest rates were high and prices low, you got one of the best investments ever. They are conservative and worth a whole lot more than you paid for them.

There can be times when putting a lot of your assets into bonds makes sense; but now, after a 30-year boom in bonds, is probably not the right time. Going all in for bonds and Treasuries in 1990 would have been great. If you did that, you did very well. Just ask Bill Gross, the bond king.

But you didn't, and now most of the bond funds I look at aren't beating the returns of fixed-index annuities, which, as we've seen, offer a lot more income. Even the smartest investors in bonds— like Bill Gross or Bond God Jeff Gundlach—over the past three decades say the next decade is likely to be different.

The key is not just to diversify the assets within your portfolio, but rather to diversify your investing strategies, as John Mauldin says.

We may see the inevitable cracks in the bond market as rates rise. During the long recovery from the 2008 recession, a lot of companies took out excessive amounts of debt fueled by private equity firms looking for profit. The companies generally issued bonds to spread the debt load on to investors. That was perfect at low, low interest rates. But as rates rise, bond funds that own these issues will lose money, bond prices overall will fall, and there's a real risk that a chain of events, such as an unexpected bankruptcy or two, will fuel fear and panic in the market.

We've already had a taste.

In October 2017, a company called Iconix, which owned global brands including Umbro and Lee Cooper, unexpectedly announced that it had lost a contract with Walmart for its Danskin brand, among other bad news, and saw its stock and bond price tumble 40 percent in one day. Bonds issued by the once hugely popular toy retailer Toys "R" Us tumbled just before the company declared bankruptcy in September 2017.

MUNIS TO THE RESCUE?

Okay, so corporate bonds, especially junk bonds with great rates of interest, are risky. But what about municipal bonds? They're conservative and tax-free, right?

Many are. But if you get a little too greedy and buy bonds of municipalities like Detroit or Flint, Michigan, or maybe Puerto Rico, which looked great in the brochures, you're in trouble now.

The point is that any part of government, struggling under huge debt and perhaps local mismanagement or a disaster, could default and simply not pay the interest on the bonds. It's happened before, and it may happen again.

Many income-oriented investors may be reaching into Europe, Japan, and other countries for bonds. Yields can be higher overseas, but the risks are far greater and decisions at the Fed may put pressure on bond prices as rates rise.

Exchange-traded bond funds (ETFs) are the most popular retirement investments today, because they seem safe and offer good yields.

But . . .

A lot of these bond ETFs are essentially unmanaged with no contractual guarantees. They are passive, meaning no one is watching them. What happens when people start fleeing for safety and would rather buy bank CDs? Could we see another quick crash like in 2008? Maybe, so why take the chance?

Municipal bonds (munis) have certain benefits because the interest rate is set, and many are tax-free. But there is also interest-rate risk and political risk, so do your homework.

THE RATINGS TRAP

A lot of investors rely heavily on bond ratings from companies like Morningstar. They use a rating system from one to five stars, with five being the best. They put a whole lot of bonds into each category.

So, no problem. Load up on 5-star bonds and you'll be safe and rich. Not so fast.

A recent study showed that a number of bond funds actually performed worse than the market as a whole after they got their 5-star ratings. This is no disrespect to Morningstar, just a heads-up that you've got to look beyond the rating when you or your advisor does the research.

In part, that's because the big ratings agencies use a bell-curve distribution, which means that for Morningstar, the top 10 percent of all bond funds get five stars, the next 22.5 percent get four stars, the next 35 percent get three, then the next 22.5 percent receives two, and the bottom 10 percent gets one.

These classes all contain vast numbers of funds, and every single one of them needs to be checked out before you put your money into it. As with most things in life, you get what you pay for, but you might not necessarily want to pay the premium for a 5-star fund when a solid 3-star might be better for you.

An article in the *Wall Street Journal* in October 2017, by Kirstin Grind, Tom McGinty, and Sarah Krouse headlined "The Morningstar Mirage," found that the star rating system was a poor predictor of future results for even 5-star bonds. In some cases, they found that these top-rated bonds fell to 2-star or even 1-star rankings after they reached the pinnacle.

What happens is that money pours into newly minted 5-star funds, and it's almost like the kiss of death. It's like the old *Sports Illustrated* curse—when your football team or its star quarterback appears on the cover, it's all over. Well, that "curse" doesn't always happen, and 5-star funds don't always crash, but it's good to beware.

Morningstar took detailed and vehement exception to the *Journal* story, but I think the central fact, which they actually agree with, is that the ratings system is backward-looking, not forward-looking. It's not supposed to predict future results, but that's how many misuse the rating. Let's look at this a little more deeply. It's important.

Investors everywhere think a 5-star rating means a fund will be a top performer. The *Journal* tested the ratings by examining thousands of funds dating back to 2003, shortly after Morningstar began its current system. Funds that earned high star ratings attract most investor dollars. But only 12 percent of 5-star funds did well enough over the next five years to earn a top rating for that period. Ten percent perform so poorly that they were branded with a rock-bottom 1-star rating. How could that be?

Some of it may be managers resting on their laurels—or just doing next year what they did this year—confident that they can market their fund using that 5-star rating for years to come. This is serious! Billions of dollars hang in the balance. Nearly every asset manager in the world pays Morningstar for data services, and some 250,000 advisors rely on the data. This means that Morningstar's analysis and ratings influence investment decisions for a vast landscape of retirement plans and brokerage accounts.

Morningstar says it has never claimed its star rating suggests how funds will perform in the future. The star system is strictly backward-looking, only assessing past performance. The system works well when it's used as intended, as a first-stage screen that helps identify lower-cost, lower-risk funds with good long-term performance. It's not meant to be used in isolation or as a predictive measure. Morningstar is an organization that's done a relatively good job shedding light on an industry that often cloaks itself in opacity. Investors of all classes are better off to have the information they put out into the world. The problems come in when this information is used incorrectly.

The reality is that many investors treat the stars as a guide to future performance, and that is not the case; so that's why, when searching for bonds, you've got to get out of bond jail and not look at these stars as a rating system to predict future growth.

Okay, so we probably can't just buy 5-star bonds and live happily ever after.

Instead, be leery of bonds, though not afraid. They've had a great 30-year run; but in an era of rising interest rates and rising budget deficits, they're not a panacea.

Let's also look at the difference between owning a bond—say, a New Jersey General Obligation Fund bond—versus owning a bond fund that might have NJ bonds in it along with a lot of other stuff. The biggest difference is what happens in the event the market goes down and investors lose confidence on a broad front. That bond fund may lose value as investors head for the exits, even if the NJ bonds are fine. That's not a problem if you own the bonds yourself.

BOND LADDERING

Another strategy is bond laddering. Bond laddering is a fixed-income investment strategy where the investor buys individual bonds of various maturities, like buying bank CDs with varying maturities, but without locking up all your money. You might buy 3-year, 5-year, 10-year, and 30-year bonds, including Treasury bonds of these durations. The shorter duration bonds may offer more liquidity to take advantage of future situations if rates rise.

Let me emphasize that nothing—not even bonds—is foolproof. Some thought Puerto Rican bonds were fine a few years ago. If you bought and held these guys before financial mismanagement led to huge budget deficits and the island defaulted, you're now out of luck.

But surely Treasury bills, bonds, and notes, backed by the full faith and credit of the US government, are safe? They are certainly safer than Puerto Rican bonds, but you buy that safety with lower returns. That's not always bad, but retirement is a 30-year or more deal. If you're going to depend on this income for 30 years, maybe 1 percent or 2 percent isn't going to be much help. It's safe enough, but it's not going to buy you much, especially if inflation picks up.

Bonds have performed very well the last 30 years because interest rates were going down and stayed near zero. If you had a 50/50 stock and bond portfolio, Treasuries were one of the best things you could buy. But in the past couple of years bond funds have been pretty much on a seesaw. When the market expects interest rates to go down, the bond funds go up. When the market expects interest rates to go up, the bond funds go down.

But what happens if your stocks go down and your bonds go down at the same time? The conventional wisdom says you just suck it up.

Wall Street and most investing professionals and almost every TV commercial having to do with retirement planning—all tout diversification. Surely it must be the answer to all your risk.

They usually mean put 50 percent of your money in stocks and 50 percent in bonds.

Wrong.

As I said before, the pie is the lie.

Instead of that pie, I recommend two things: diversifying asset strategies, not just asset allocation; and AIM, a new paradigm.

The rest of the book will fill in the details, but AIM stands for:

- *Annuities* for your nest egg
- *Insurance* for your new money
- *Managed* money in stocks for the old money

No bonds.

Now, when I say annuities, I am not recommending you annuitize. Annuitization essentially gives control to the issuing insurance company forever, in exchange for a higher stream of income. While not wrong for everyone if income is your goal, in this acronym is the idea that the income needs of your first 10 years of retirement should be met by something that gives you a pension or an annual stream of income—ergo annuity—for life. You shouldn't take a chance with your income needs during the first 10 years in retirement, because you may not be able to make up for a lost decade in the stock market. Think of a *now* and *later* candy: the annuity gives you money *now* to live on; the insurance offers income *later*; and the managed money in equities hedge you a bit from inflation and allow you to get the longer-term returns the equity markets afford. Let's see how it works.

MEET DANIEL

Daniel is a 60-year-old divorced real estate agent. He wants to work another 10 years. He's got $800,000 in savings and figures to generate another $300,000 in free cash over the next decade.

He came to me wanting to put all of that $800,000 in the stock market "to take a shot" at getting past $1 million. We pointed out that likely future returns, based on solid history, indicate he might get up to $832,000, or down to under $700,000, within the next year if he depended on the stock market.

TAKE AIM

Rather than risk everything right now in a bull market, we took AIM. This approach blends objectives of future income while allowing the investor opportunity in the stock market, too:

A. We took $400,000 of his $800,000 and bought him a fixed annuity with an income rider that's contractually guaranteed to pay him $50,000 a year if he defers taking income for 10 years. When he starts collecting Social Security of about $39,000 a year, that's going to give him an *annuity* (after all, Social Security is a type of annuity) of nearly $90,000 a year to live on, which he says is plenty. Now, he has so much less stress as we invest the difference in the stock market.

I.   We bought him a 10-Pay cash-value life insurance policy for which he pays $30,000 in premiums a year. The premiums are guaranteed never to go up and to be concluded at the end of 10 years. Under this policy, he can take out—based on current dividends—$21,000 a year between the ages of 70 and 85, adding to the $90,000 we've just guaranteed him. Plus, he gets additional benefits: life insurance to make sure his kids inherit his money tax-free, and the ability to spend the death benefit while he's alive in the form of an accelerated death benefit (ADB). An ADB allows you to spend a large percentage of your death benefit if you ever have a stroke, cancer, Alzheimer's, dementia, or any other seriously debilitating illness. Even after living on $90K plus the $21K from the insurance, he will likely have $300,000 in ADB in the event of long-term care or for his kids when he dies.

M.   We took the $400,000 he didn't put into the annuity into a managed small cap exchange-traded fund linked to the S&P 600 index for higher growth potential.

Notice anything? No bonds! Just growth and income.

ALAN AND ASHLEY AGAIN

It turns out that the portfolio we assembled for Alan and Ashley looks nothing at all like Harry Markowitz's Nobel Prize–winning pie charts.

With Alan's $600,000, we sold his dog stock (the government property trust) and bought them a fixed-index annuity. We got them income from a reverse mortgage on their fully paid-up $350,000 suburban house.

All in all, they're getting about $100,000 a year, and that's not going to go away. The safety is worth a whole lot more than any extra gain they *might* have made. It's also more than they would have made by slavishly following a 60-year-old investing formula.

ACTION STEPS

- There's nothing wrong with investing in bonds as part of a multi-income stream spend-down strategy.
- Don't worry about meeting specific percentage goals for stocks or bonds in your portfolio.
- Having a strategy and sticking to it is great, but the strategy itself needs to be flexible and tailored.

10

REALITY CHECK

FORGET
DOLLAR COST
AVERAGING.

MEET JEREMY

Jeremy loved General Electric stock. He thought Jack Welch was the greatest CEO he had ever seen. He didn't care for Welch's successor, Jeff Immelt. Still, he believed in the company; he and his wife, Susan, had a GE refrigerator, washing machine, and dryer.

Jeremy first bought 500 shares of GE stock just before September 11, 2001, at around $30 a share. In the stock bloodbath that followed the downing of the World Trade Center in New York, GE fell sharply down to about $15 in 2003, so his $15,000 original investment was now worth about $7,500. Jeremy, still liking GE and those appliances and executives, figured this was the perfect opportunity to buy more. He bought another 500 shares at $15, so he now owned 1,000 shares for which he had paid a total of $22,500, or an average cost of $22.50 a share.

He faithfully held on even after the 2007 financial crash, when GE shares plunged to just over $5 a share. On the way down to that low, George bought 1,000 shares at $10 each. He now owned 2,000 shares for which he had paid $32,500, thus bringing his average cost down to $16.25—a lot better, he figured, than his initial $30 a share, poised to go back up and net him a hefty profit. If GE could just get back to the $30 a share, Jeremy's nest egg would be worth $60,000, nearly a 50 percent gain!

And indeed it got there at the end of 2017, buoyed by the healthy worldwide economy and some well-received corporate reorganization and sell-offs. Jeremy was pleased with his gains, and he even felt richer. But alas, the gains were on paper only. He didn't sell any of the stock, and its value plunged back down to $13. His 2,000 shares, which cost him $32,500, were now worth $30,000. He had tied up a whole bunch of money for 17 years for a negative return!

DOLLAR-LOST AVERAGING

As Jeremy's sad saga shows, the popular investing theory of dollar cost averaging can become dollar-lost averaging if you're not careful.

The theory is simple and sounds great. . . .

If a stock you've invested in goes down, buy more shares at the cheaper price, divide the total amount you've now invested by the number of shares you now own, and *voilà!* your average cost is somewhere above the current price, so you feel better.

For instance, let's say you bought 100 shares of Acme Co. stock at $100 a share a year ago. Acme turned out to be a dog and is now trading at $50 a share. Instead of getting out and taking a $5,000 loss, you buy another 100 shares at $50.

You now own 200 shares that cost you $15,000, so your average cost is $75 a share. Great! Better than $50 a share. But the problem is that you can't sell them for $75 a share—people are only offering $50. If they go down further, you're even more stuck. You've now maybe got 200 shares of a $25 stock, worth $5,000. You're down 67 percent!

If they go back up to $100, you're basically back to even for no gain, but with increased exposure to the next downturn. (You own more shares.)

If you happen to use dollar cost averaging in a rising market, you'll be okay, but will probably miss out on better returns elsewhere.

If you use dollar cost averaging in a down market, you're screwed. You've discovered the woes of negative compounding. Don't go there.

Although DCA investing can help the average investor deal with volatility, it is not a panacea. Imagine having the discipline to never sell for 10 straight years (from January 2000–December 2009) into an S&P 500 index fund. Ben Carlson shares an example of DCA not paying off:

> If you started dollar cost averaging $500/month into the S&P 500 in January of 2000, by December of 2009 you would have invested $60,000 in total. This strategy would have netted you a whopping $64k and change, not much more than the amount saved. By way of comparison, simply investing that same $500/month in one-month t-bills would have given you more than $67k.
>
> It's no secret the lost decade of the 2000s was a difficult one for investors considering on a total return basis the S&P 500 was down more than 9% over a ten year period (so averaging in helped a little but not much).

Emerging markets are working through their own lost decade(-ish) at the moment. From November of 2007 through September of 2018 the MSCI EM Index is up just 5.5% in total. Over that time the S&P is up nearly 140% while lowly one-month t-bills have risen 4.9%.

Using the same DCA strategy of investing $500/ month in EM over this time would have been an investment of $65,500. The ending balance would now be just shy of $85k.[1]

I understand that this may be a misrepresentative sample. However, Vanguard studied 1,021 different 12-month rolling periods and found that DCA underperformed lump-sum investing two-thirds of the time.[2]

Diversifying over time by dollar cost averaging, Carlson says, "won't always protect you from a bad market environment. This is yet another reason it pays to diversify across asset classes, market capitalizations, and investment strategies."[3]

Once again, ask yourself: Why do you want to continually put money into something that's underperforming?

It's much better to take a hit and move on to stock in companies that have a brighter future. All the time Jeremy slavishly backed a faltering General Electric (maker of refrigerators and then-owner of NBC), Facebook, Apple, Netflix, and Google were changing both how we all live and soaring on the stock market. Jeremy didn't even need to predict the rise of all these companies. One ETF or fund would've done nicely.

And, of course, if you just don't want to get into picking individual stocks, put the money into lower-cost mutual funds or ETF trading strategies that do the picking for you.

Just don't get caught throwing good money after a bad stock.

ACTION STEPS

- When a favorite stock of yours goes down, it's tempting to buy more, lowering your average cost per share.
- This is a good strategy when the stock goes back up, if you're prepared to sell.
- It's a disaster if the stock plunges further or never goes back up. You're stuck with more shares at a lower price.

PART III

SPEND 'TIL THE END

11

REALITY CHECK

DIVERSIFICATION COULD
LEAD TO DI-WORSIFICATION.

MEET TONY

Tony is a 58-year-old divorced urban planner in St. Louis. He's a big Cardinals fan and goes fly-fishing with a bunch of buddies nearly every weekend.

Tony has a $500,000 nest egg and reads a lot of financial planning books and websites. If there's one thing he knows about finances, it's that he's got to diversify.

For the past 20 years, he's put 60 percent of his money in stock funds and 40 percent in bond funds. Every year, he looks at the balance and asks his financial advisor to get everything back to 60/40 if it's fallen out of line.

Tony is happy with the average 3.5 percent return he has gained as a result. It's better than inflation, he figures. He doesn't want to be greedy, and he doesn't want to take any big risks. Besides, he's *diversified*.

Conventional investing wisdom is that everybody should be like Tony and diversify their investments with, say, a 60 percent share of stocks and a 40 percent share of bonds. As with most conventional wisdom, it's not completely wrong. But in many specific cases, relying on this sort of rote diversification can be limiting. In some cases, it can even be harmful.

But what if I tell you that you can do a lot better than Tony's 3.5 percent, at little or no extra risk, if you shake off the 60/40 handcuffs?

DON'T DI-WORSIFY

I'm a believer in diversification, not di-worsification. You want to diversify income streams in retirement. Especially in our current era of a very highly valued stock market, you need to look at other kinds of investments. Not just bonds, but also alternatives like real estate and even commodities such as gold, silver, or cryptocurrencies. This all needs to be done carefully and with trusted advice, not a tip from Uncle Harry or a tweet from somebody you don't know.

Diversification becomes di-worsification when it's done by rote, not according to a careful plan, based on your model. No tips from Uncle Harry.

The fund giant T. Rowe Price did a study of four typical retirees and their chances of outliving their savings over 30 years. Everybody started with $500,000 and retired on January 1, 2000. The study used a sophisticated analysis of real returns for the first 10 years and projections for the next 20. Fifty-five percent of the money was invested in stocks and 45 percent in equities.

Based on the initial probability analysis, these investors had an 89 percent chance of sustaining—that is, keeping their heads above water—over the next 30 years.

But the 2000 and 2002 and 2007 and 2009 bear markets wreaked havoc on their potential success. It all looked pretty good in 2000, just as things look pretty good now. For the last 10 years, a 55/45 portfolio would have done okay, about a 4 percent return with very little inflation. However, if we repeat a decade like 2000 to 2010, we could be in for trouble. By the end of the bear market (September 2002, for example), the 89 percent odds of sustaining retirement fell to just 46 percent. Those odds were largely restored by the five-year bull market that followed, but then they fell again after the 2007–2008 recession to a paltry 6 percent!

NOT MUCH CHANCE

A 6 percent chance of success. Wow.

Let's say you start out with $500,000 in retirement today. A bear market might reduce that $500,000 to $250,000. If that happens, would you stick with a 55/45 investment plan? Really? In real life, most investors do not stick with that plan and with their advisors. It's the same mentality as the dollar cost averagers we met in the previous chapter.

So, what do you do?

Lots of people simply tightened their belts during the recession. They reduced withdrawals and didn't eat out as much and deferred vacations and didn't buy that new car.

A lot of people overreacted to the stock-market decline and moved a lot more money into bonds and bond funds. Great, but then they missed the equity recovery and were stuck with low-yielding bonds.

DON'T SCRIMP!

But if you work your whole life, do you really want to reduce your withdrawals and duck in your head when you need the money the most? You may not be around in 10 years, so why scrimp?

Nobody times the market perfectly, but just like those dollar cost averagers, fleeing to bonds right after a stock decline may be throwing good money after bad. The answer is to get more conservative during good times, to better weather the bad times. That may mean a reversal to 55 percent or even 60 percent bonds. Look at more conservative instruments now rather than later. Lots of people think they are protecting their money just by having a lot of different kinds of investments. Big- and small-cap stocks, international stock, municipal bonds, Treasuries, and whatnot.

Let's use our good old example of $1 million saved for retirement.

How are you going to convert what you have to a stream of income without going broke? The answer is something most people don't think about, or even know is a thing, and which old-school financial planners basically ignore: a spend-down strategy.

Most advisors will tell you: "Okay, you have a million dollars saved for retirement invested in a 60 percent stock, 40 percent bond portfolio. All you have to do is withdraw 4 percent a year—no more!—and you're going to be okay for life."

Wrong. This is a fine strategy as long as those stock and bond investments hold up. You've pared your spending to $40,000 a year and the market has basically grown enough so you can keep going forever and still have that million to leave to your kids when you die.

The old wisdom works until there's a major stock-market downturn, like the one in 2007–2008. As I write this, we're in one of the longest bull markets ever, and they don't last forever.

You don't want to base your whole life on someone's prediction. What if they're wrong?

YOU NEED A STRATEGY

That's why a spend-down strategy matters. We'll start with that mythical $1 million. If you have a million dollars in a portfolio, you take half a million and put that in something conservative. It might be a bond fund, it might be a fixed annuity, it might be Treasury bonds. This is the money you're going to spend down. Use it for food, rent, movies, that trip to Umbria. Go out to dinner. Buy those Yankees season tickets you've wanted since you were 10.

Enjoy life!

Put the other $500,000 in a low-fee portfolio of stock and bond funds, with as much risk as you're comfortable with. You could go for high growth, you could go for a small cap value fund and let it rip. If the managers hit it big, so do you. Even if this fund takes a dip, which it will, you're living off the more conservative stuff, and can wait for the growth fund to come back.

We're building a retirement paycheck, or a play check.

The old paradigm is dead. Here's why.

If you have a million dollars and you live on the old paradigm and we go through a market crash, you're only able to take about 2 percent out of your portfolio, according to a paper published in January 2013 by David Blanchett, Michael Finke, and Wade Pfau entitled "Low Bond Yields and Safe Portfolio Withdrawal Rates." If we go through another lost decade as we did from 2000 to 2010, you may be out of luck. You'll be miserable, and you won't have any money!

In our new system, you've got all those lovely Treasuries and fixed annuities allowing you to spend your money and enjoy your retirement. Your stock funds may take a beating, but you're not spending those right now anyway. You can wait for them to come back.

Once again, isn't the whole point for you to enjoy your retirement? Isn't the whole purpose of investing not just the numbers on your statement, but the enjoyment of spending money with the people you love and the causes you love? You work 40 years of your life and you accumulate, you scrimp, you save, and from age 25 to age 65 you work hard. Then you retire at 65 and you drop dead at 66 because something happens. Or you die in your early 70s. We don't know how long we have on this earth, so there should be a certain reserve of money we can enjoy while we're here.

TWO PORTFOLIOS

A tale of two portfolios may help elucidate this spend-down strategy.

Let's assume you have that $1 million and you put $500,000 in a 10-year CD, or a 10-year fixed annuity earning 3.5 percent. You're going to withdraw $50,000 a year as soon as you retire and take that vacation to Italy you've always wanted. Don't wait until you're 75. Do it now.

Take out that $50,000 every year for 11 or 12 years, until it's exhausted. That's on top of Social Security and anything else you've got coming in.

By now, you're perhaps 77. We didn't talk about what you're going to do with the other $500,000. But we've gotten you happily through the first 12 years of retirement with at least $500,000 still intact in your stock fund. Because you had half of your money off the market merry-go-round, you slept better, you didn't watch CNBC every day, and instead you had time to look into the beautiful eyes of your children and grandchildren. However, 12 years into retirement, it is spent down (see next page).

But let's say you did nothing but put that other $500,000 into a S&P 600 small cap index fund. Now, for numbers' sake, we are using the results of the S&P 600 from 1928 to 1948. I realize that you cannot invest directly in an index, but today there are many ETFs and index funds that can link to the asset class of small cap

Year	Annual Payment	Account Balance BOY	Account Balance EOY	Other	True Value
1	($50,000)	$500,000	$465,750	$0	$465,750
2	($50,000)	$465,750	$430,301	$0	$430,301
3	($50,000)	$430,301	$393,612	$0	$393,6120
4	($50,000)	$393,312	$355,638	$0	$355,638
5	($50,000)	$355,638	$316,336	$0	$316,336
6	($50,000)	$316,336	$275,657	$0	$275,657
7	($50,000)	$275,657	$233,555	$0	$233,555
8	($50,000)	$233,555	$189,980	$0	$189,980
9	($50,000)	$189,980	$144,879	$0	$144,879
10	($50,000)	$144,879	$98,200	$0	$98,200
11	($50,000)	$98,200	$49,887	$0	$49,887
12	($50,000)	$49,887	($117)	$0	($117)

passively. Let's say you put your money into the market before a crash like we haven't seen since 1928.

Indeed, if you had been in the market in 1928, you would have had one good year—1928—where you made 39 percent, and then for the next four years you would have lost 30 percent, then 31 percent, then 47 percent, and then 10 percent. That $500,000 would be down to $149,146, including a 1 percent fee and not counting taxes. Yikes!

The conventional wisdom would have told you to take your losses and get out.

But remember, our strategy says you buy and hold for 11 or 12 years. Even in the Great Depression, the market came back in 1933. Even after accounting for spending down $50,000 a year from year 12 to year 20 in our chart (see next page)—we are using the S&P 600 small cap index—your principal would still be $1,215,628. Not a bad spend-down strategy. And that was during arguably the worst-ever time to invest.

Year	Balance BOY	Interest Rate	Annual Payment	Mgt. Fee	Misc. Fee	Annual Term	Annual Tax	Balance EOY
1	$500,000	39.64%	$0	($5,000)	$0	$0	($16,352)	$674,867
2	$674,867	-30.75%	$0	($6,749)	$0	$0	$0	$462,471
3	$426,471	-31.23%	$0	($4,265)	$0	$0	$0	$314,861
4	$314,861	-47.40%	$0	($3,149)	$0	$0	$0	$163,961
5	$163,961	-10.26%	$0	($1,640)	$0	$0	$0	$145,667
6	$145,667	125.63%	$0	($1,457)	$0	$0	($15,098)	$310,284
7	$310,284	18.25%	$0	($3,103)	$0	$0	($4,672)	$358,570
8	$358,570	76.69%	$0	($3,586)	$0	$0	($22,686)	$604,535
9	$604,535	48.92%	$0	($6,045)	$0	$0	($24,398)	$866,873
10	$866,873	-48.74%	$0	($8,669)	$0	$0	$0	$439,916
11	$439,916	43.39%	$0	($4,399)	$0	$0	($15,748)	$608,739
12	$608,739	0.70%	(-$50,000)	($6,087)	$0	$0	($322)	$556,198
13	$556,198	-1.82%	(-$50,000)	($5,562)	$0	$0	$0	$491,525
14	$491,525	-10.96%	(-$50,000)	($4,915)	$0	$0	$0	$388,757
15	$388,757	29.20%	(-$50,000)	($3,888)	$0	$0	($8,148)	$424,503
16	$424,503	55.09%	(-$50,000)	($4,245)	$0	$0	($16,998)	$557,235
17	$557,235	40.12%	(-$50,000)	($5,572)	$0	$0	($16,772)	$686,157
18	$686,157	59.73%	(-$50,000)	($6,862)	$0	$0	($31,323)	$973,851
19	$973,851	-10.26%	(-$50,000)	($9,739)	$0	$0	$0	$820,324
20	$820,324	-2.49%	(-$50,000)	($8,203)	$0	$0	$0	$743,144

Deferred CG Tax: $0

Totals:			($450,000)	($103,493)	$0	$0	($172,518)	$743,144

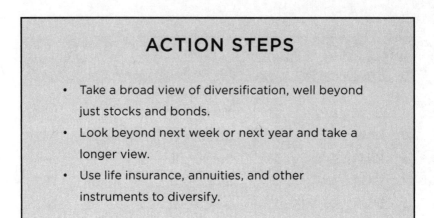

ACTION STEPS

- Take a broad view of diversification, well beyond just stocks and bonds.
- Look beyond next week or next year and take a longer view.
- Use life insurance, annuities, and other instruments to diversify.

12

REALITY CHECK

RETIRE IN THE ZERO TAX BRACKET. A WELL-THOUGHT-OUT SPEND-DOWN STRATEGY WILL GET YOU THERE.

MEET PHILIP AND ROBIN

Philip managed a chain of clothing stores in San Francisco, and his wife, Robin, was a six-figure personnel recruiter in Silicon Valley.

They have $2 million in IRAs. They've made it! They've reached the top of the mountain. But just as Mount Everest climbers have said, "It's not climbing that's the hardest part; it's coming down."

Philip and Robin need a strategy on what to do with the money they've already earned. So if you were a good boy or girl like Philip and Robin, how do you manage your nest egg? If you're just starting out and can't imagine amassing $2 million for retirement, I'm sharing this story not to depress you, but *so that you may begin with the end in mind.*

Let's say you've saved—as many people have—a large amount in your qualified retirement plan (QRP). The alphabet soup of investing. If it's got a letter behind it—401(k), 403(b), 457(b)—it's part of our tax code. If the government created it, can it really be that good a thing? 401(k)s and other qualified retirement plans are like drivers in the game of golf. They take the ball very far. They're great in the accumulation stage, but they don't finish the game well. A putter makes a lousy driver, and a driver makes a lousy putter. QRPs are good at accumulating, but weak in the distribution phase when you have to take withdrawals out of your 401(k) or IRA.

Back to Philip and Robin. They have $2 million. Conventional wisdom says to take the $2 million and live on 3.5 percent—$70,000—per year. But then the government will have you take out more than that over time due to the required minimum distribution (RMD). The problem with RMDs and taking 3.5–4 percent from your IRA is that all that money goes on your tax return as ordinary income.

To recap, the problems of the RMD-only strategy:

1. You're only taking 3.5–5 percent out. You're not truly enjoying your money.
2. You're getting taxed while you live, and your heirs will pay taxes when you pass into eternity.

They're getting hit with $80,000 a year in taxes, assuming they're at a 24 percent federal-income tax level. That's 24 percent federal, plus 6 percent state. There's got to be a better way!

Philip and Robin, instead of following the interest-only strategy, which means they are taxed when they live and taxed when they die, did something called a strategic rollout.

They take $200,000 out of their IRAs every year, draining it in 10 years. They pay the tax on that, which is $60,000 a year for 10 years, and they sock away $140,000 each year in a 10-Pay life insurance policy with a dividend-paying mutual company. At the end of 10 years, they then can pull out. They get to the zero-percent tax bracket by paying taxes every year for 10 years, and then in year 11 and following they'll be in the zero-percent tax bracket because they will take out $98,000 per year tax-free, and from year 11 of retirement to year 25, all the while, the 10-Pay has a death benefit to protect them in the event of a chronic or terminal illness.

Now you might be thinking: "How does a couple with $2 million get into the zero tax bracket?" It's because they've spent down their IRA, taken that money out of the taxable envelope, and put it into the tax-free envelope. The only income that would remain would be Social Security income. Philip gets $15,000 a year from Social Security; Robin gets $30,000. So based on the provisional income formula, they would even get money tax-free from Social Security, whereas most couples who have Social Security would be taxed on 85 percent of it. Because they don't have taxable streams of income, because they repositioned the 2 percent they had in tax-deferred into tax-advantaged never-taxed accounts, cash value inside a life insurance policy does not count against them in the provisional income formula. Not only are they not paying tax on the $98,000, they will not pay any tax on the Social Security check they're receiving. Normally, married couples having greater than $44,000 of extra income pay income tax on up to 85 percent of their Social Security income.

So there are no more RMDs, there are more tax on Social Security income after year 10, they're protecting their family with the death benefit, and they're enjoying their money in years 11 to 30 of retirement by taking tax-free loans out of their insurance contract.

SPEND AND SAVE

The point of a spend-down strategy is to divide your portfolio into two equal parts.

One part is going to be something pretty conservative. In previous financial planning orthodoxy, this would go into bonds. You earn 3 percent or 4 percent a year and try to live off of that.

But in our system, this half is the part you're literally going to spend down, taking, say, 10 percent a year to live and do what you want. We usually recommend an annuity that will pay you a 3 percent to 4 percent return but you're going to withdraw 10 percent of the principal for your expenses in the first 10 years of retirement. If you have $1 million, half of that goes into a no-fee annuity and you withdraw $50,000 a year. A fixed annuity that gives a 3 percent or 4 percent yield stretches out your money from 10 years to 12 or 14. You invest the other $500,000 in stocks and don't touch it.

The main difference between this and past strategies is that not only are you getting enough to spend each year, you're still allowing yourself to take advantage of the compound-interest curve on your equities. You're stretching out your assets. It also allows you to take some risk for higher returns on the half of the money that's in stocks, letting you ride out market ups and downs without volatility getting you down.

If you have a spend-down strategy, you can have two accounts of differing natures. One account, the spend-down account, is for the money that you're going to need now. The stock-market part gives you income later. The spend-down part hedges you against equity market risks. The stock-market bucket hedges you against inflation risk. It's like the Now and Later candy I mentioned earlier.

A good spend-down strategy includes not just which stuff you spend down, but the order in which you spend them down. You may have certificates of deposit, treasuries, cash, some tax-free bonds and some taxable bonds, fixed annuities, and an IRA. But just like a math equation, the order in which you perform each operation can change the result.

Let's take a simple example. Let's say you have $500,000 for retirement, with half in an IRA and half in cash. The best strategy is to put your IRA money into cash-like, safe investments like IRA CDs or IRA fixed annuities, and put your cash into stock mutual funds.

When you reach retirement age, the correct spend-down order is: stock funds first, IRA second. That's because the income from the stock funds is going to be taxed at capital-gains rates, not as ordinary income. For many taxpayers, the ordinary rate is around 35 percent and the capital-gains rate is about 20 percent.

Also, if you spend the stock-fund money in your first few years of retirement, that will tide you over until age 70½. That's the age that the government makes you take money out of your IRAs, the so-called required minimum distribution, typically 4 percent of your IRA funds. So at that point, you shift over to the IRA money, which you've got to take anyway.

With any luck, while you've been spending down the first half of your assets, the second half, the part that's been invested in stocks, has been growing. Historically, it's no stretch to think that $500,000, say, would double in 10 to 14 years to $1 million. *Voilà!* You're back to your original $1 million, while having lived nicely for 10 years. You can start the process all over again!

DON'T SCREW IT UP!

I've found across the board that clients who come to me with $500,000 to $800,000 in assets accumulated over a lifetime of work basically don't want to screw it up. They have less of a stomach for risk, and that's where a sound spend-down strategy comes in, which utilizes every available tax break and safe investment strategy from annuities to life insurance.

I've also found that the most scared of any of my clients are those who've already got between $2 million and $4 million in assets. They are the most dangerous in terms of thinking they know all about sound investing and, oddly, seem the most vulnerable to investment scams, especially if they are older.

One of my clients had half his assets, about $2 million, all in PepsiCo. stock. That was great for a while, not so great now, and no way to run a retirement.

A better strategy to invest $4 million is to put $2 million in a balanced stock portfolio (not all Pepsi) and the rest in volatility buffers like a no-load, fixed-interest, no-fee annuity. This would allow you to spend about $200,000 a year for the next 15 years with virtually no risk and without touching the other $2 million in stocks. Meanwhile, if that stock portfolio makes 7 percent a year net of fees, the total gets back to $4 million in 10 years and you can spend it down all over again! What did Einstein say about compound interest?

Sadly, I see many clients with substantial assets who think they can prosper in hedge funds, private equity, gold, commodities, and whatnot—it all looks great on Fox Business Network!—but who eventually get outplayed by the pros.

Russ is a retired journalist now in his 80s, with dozens of grandchildren who light up his days. By the time he was 50, he had $2 million invested in blue chip stocks, a strategy his advisors thought was great. But those blue chips included General Electric, General Motors, Lucent, and a bunch of Baby Bells. He pretty much got every pick wrong. No FAANG for Russ. In 30 years, that $2 million became $70,000. There's nothing wrong with high-yield stocks, but their prices can drop, and have dropped, 30–40 percent, and dividends tend to get cut when companies get into trouble.

Russ also, of course, had no spend-down strategy. If he had, even with those horrible picks, he'd still have at least the $1 million in less-risky investments, and arguably a lot more.

None of these things can beat a good tax-smart spend-down strategy in the long term.

For example, most people have stocks growing tax-free in their IRAs or 401(k)s and tax-free bonds in their investment accounts outside their IRAs. But that's all wrong, because eventually you've got to spend down the IRA to meet the government's mandatory minimum drawdown rules and pay tax on the total amount.

The correct plan is to have about half your assets in an IRA and half outside it. The non-risky stuff like bond ladders, no-fee annuities, Treasury bills, or very low-risk bonds should be in the IRA. The risky stuff like stocks should be outside it. You'll pay taxes on the dividends, but not on the capital growth until you sell them—and you won't need to sell them! Your equities will grow without worry because you won't need to liquidate them in a downturn. You don't need to time the market. You can retire at ease.

This is the opposite of most conventional advice. That entails growing your nest egg enough each year so you can spend 4 percent of it without making a dent in the capital. You're clipping bond coupons or spending stock dividends. This is great, but nobody can actually do it because markets go up and down—and with this strategy, down is really down. If you didn't realize that right after 9/11 in 2001 and right after the 2007 crash were the right times to buy stocks, you're not going to pull off the 4 percent rule (see next chapter).

Most people come to me with a decent enough pie, but they have no idea that they indeed can both eat some of it and have a big pie if they have a good spend-down strategy.

The best way to establish a spend-down strategy is to find an asset class (or classes) that you can draw down for the first 10 years of retirement, with an investment portfolio growing 3–5 percent a year to replenish the spend-down asset.

ACTION STEPS

- How and when to spend your nest egg is as important as making it in the first place.
- A conservative spend-down strategy lets you use all the available tax laws to your benefit.
- This strategy will let you spend money on things you enjoy or need, while still maintaining reserves for your retirement.

13

CONSERVATIVE WITHDRAWAL STRATEGIES CAN GENERATE 30 PERCENT MORE INCOME FOR RETIREMENT. FORGET THE 4 PERCENT RULE.

MEET SARAH

Sarah majored in marketing at Northwestern and then plunged into the real world, applying to every marketing job she heard about or spotted online. She decided not to limit herself to Indianapolis, her hometown, or Chicago, and expanded her search nationwide. Luckily, she got offered a great entry-level position at a marketing firm in Boston. Sarah had to pack up and start a new life in a new city, but she eventually found traction in her job and started to excel and impress clients as well as her management.

After a few lateral moves, Sarah landed her dream job, as a marketing executive for Gillette, leading a five-person team working on new products for women. Her personal life progressed as well: she met a great guy, got married, settled down, and managed to fit two children—one boy and one girl—into her life. Buying a modest house was always a dream of hers, and she found the perfect 3,000-square-foot modern home in a nice Boston suburb. Supporting her family—her husband was a noble but underpaid high-school teacher—was always important to her, and she set aside money each month for the kids' education and her retirement. It is not always easy to remain disciplined, but she did, working hard to ensure that she did. Month in and month out, she followed her targeted saving goals.

The day finally came for Sarah to retire and enjoy the pot of gold at the end of her work rainbow. Her team threw her a small party at work, with cake and bad red wine. A few days prior to this party, Sarah and her husband sat down with their financial advisor and had an extensive meeting to discuss retirement spending.

That is when she first heard about the 4 percent rule. It made enough sense, and she had trusted her financial advisor to steer her in the right direction. So she agreed to abide by the 4 percent rule, which indicates that when you reach your retirement years, you annually spend no more than 4 percent of the money you have set aside. It is a way to budget your hard-saved money and allow you to ration appropriately. It was 2007, and Sarah's nest egg had grown into something that could support her and her husband until the end.

The first few months of retirement went off without a hitch. Sarah was thoughtful about spending, not overindulging, doing her best to be considerate about the money she had set aside. By the end of 2007, she had withdrawn and lived off $75,000, which is about 4 percent of her retirement nest egg. She nailed it. She felt satisfied in her quality of living at this level and felt confident that she could proceed ahead in this manner. Little did she know that the next two years would be two of the most challenging of her life.

Since she had followed the recommendation of her financial advisor, she put much of her wealth in mutual funds and the stock market. It always seemed like a prudent investment, and she generally netted 7–10 percent per year, enough to keep things growing. That is, in part, why withdrawing only 4 percent felt safe. She had a buffer built in, and she didn't understand what could go wrong. But 2008 was a complete catastrophe. Remaining disciplined, she only withdrew 4 percent of her savings. But, like everyone else, her investment portfolio and retirement savings were literally pounded by the stock-market crash of 2008. She had saved a little under two million dollars for her retirement, and 2008 took a big bite out of that. Factor in her 4 percent rate of withdrawal, and she lost almost 36 percent of the entire value of her portfolio—in just one tumultuous year. This was a frightening time, to say the least. A 40-year career in marketing wiped out in just one bad year.

She couldn't help but start to ask questions. Upon receiving her year-end statement balance, she immediately got on the phone and called her longtime financial advisor, searching for answers. She demanded a plan of action and a change in her investment strategies. Just one year into her retirement, she had already found herself behind the eight ball, experiencing great financial concern, and unsure as to where to go from there.

As you can imagine, this isn't just an example, but a reality for many retirees in the first decade of the 2000s. How could this happen? Easy. The issue is that *the 4 percent rule only works in prosperous markets*. By that, I mean that the market has to be rising or maintaining your gains for the 4 percent rule to actually work. For retirees in 2008, the 4 percent rule turned into the 34 percent drool, as they spent 4 percent and lost 30 percent. Just like that, a third of their retirement savings vanished into thin air.

In 1994, William P. Bengen, considered to be one of the fathers of financial planning, first articulated the 4 percent withdrawal rate as a rule of thumb. Thousands of financial advisors subscribed to this rule and spread it to the millions of individuals whose money they managed. Trillions of dollars managed by a flawed strategy. But it was easy, understandable, and seemed safe enough.

The whole 4 percent concept depends on calculating the maximum safe withdrawal rate from your portfolio. Say you have $1 million invested in a balanced stock and bond portfolio, and you want that money to last for your kids or grandkids. The rule says you should be able to live off $40,000 a year.

It caught on like wildfire, and more and more people truly bought into it. But the flaw of this strategy is that it simply doesn't account for the unforeseeable bear markets. So, if you practice the traditionally and widely accepted 4 percent rule in a bear market, you must account for the potential losses that might occur in a downward swing. Traditional planners will tell you this is a safe spending strategy. But ask any 2008 retiree just how safe they felt when making that frantic call to their advisor looking for a little accountability.

How could we not see this coming? The financial industry is one that often rests on its laurels. It remains happy and content to stay the course and continue to practice the most basic and fundamental strategies that have served it since the beginning. It would be like the car industry building cars today the same way it did in the 1950s, and then being surprised when they break down. It worked then, so why can't it work now? But times change, and so should the mechanism by which we respond to them.

There is a group of veteran and seasoned financial advisors who simply are not willing to adjust their widely accepted but outdated strategies. They subscribe to the notion that these approaches have served us for generation after generation, so what should change now? Perhaps they disregard the stock-market crashes, considerable swings that should be expected and accounted for, or the frantic calls from their clients in 2008 looking for explanations.

For whatever reason, financial advisors often feel like they are excluded from the industry change and adaptation that often defines existence vs. extinction. But as the ever-changing world of investing continues to evolve, and as people are living longer, it is now more important than ever to get this right and protect a well-earned nest egg.

If you've saved $1 million for retirement, I want you to enjoy that money. Forget the 4 percent rule. I'm going to show you lots of strategies that let you spend your money and still leave a legacy.

I am here to tell you that great financial advisors do not just implement safe-spending strategies. Moreover, they hedge against the risk that any investor will eventually recognize. That risk is like a Pac-Man, eating up all your hard-earned dollars. You must stop it dead in its tracks.

PROTECTING YOUR NEST EGG

We have to buck this trend, and it actually begins with asking important questions like:

> What happens if the market falls during my first few years of retirement?

> How will I recover from a period of spending and no saving?

> What do I do if the 4 percent rule doesn't work for me?

No one wants to talk about flawed spend-down strategies, but we must consider how these traditional practices might not always be the best ones. Think about it like this. Let's say you are a victim of a downturn. You might lose 20 percent in just one year. So now you are down 24 percent (20 percent in market loss plus 4 percent supposedly safe withdrawal rate). Factor in another 2 percent in management fees or mutual fund expenses. So, in just one year you could lose 26 percent of your nest egg. To recover over the next year, you would then need to realize almost a 50 percent return just to get close to the balance of your previous year. Sounds like an uphill battle, doesn't it? It's tough to recover from a downturn. For example, if you lose 33 percent, you need a 50 percent gain the next year just to break even.

You are probably wondering to some degree why people would subscribe to the 4 percent rule, especially after most investors practically lost their shirts in 2008. It seemed so obvious that there will inevitably be a market correction. Maybe not today or tomorrow, but it will rear its ugly head at some point in time. So, unless you plan to be yet another sheep led to the slaughter, you have to change your retirement mindset. There is a herd mentality, where advisors follow advisors and investors follow investors. They all assume that what worked for their parents and grandparents will similarly work for them.

There are three basic strategies one can choose when planning for retirement:

1. **Equities-only strategy.** Put it all into a mixture of stocks and bonds. This strategy is solely dependent on market forces that are out of your control.

2. **Investment plus annuities.** Invest in stocks but also buy an annuity, instead of buying bonds. (The annuity replaces the bond portion.) Use the annuity for your

basic monthly needs and invest the difference for growth as an inflation hedge.

3. **Investment + Income Annuity + Asset Insurance.** Buy a low-cost annuity for your minimum monthly budget, invest the difference in stocks as an inflation hedge, and purchase life insurance with the excess as asset insurance.

I like the idea of the investment plus annuity plus asset (cash-value life) insurance because it blends income with legacy with growth potential. Those who choose that option may potentially have more retirement income, a safer withdrawal rate, higher retirement confidence, and greater hedges against volatility.

As we saw in Reality Check Four, annuities have gotten a bad name, though nearly everybody would be delighted to have a guaranteed monthly income when they retire, even if they don't have a company or government pension. That's an annuity!

Annuities are perfect for your spend-down strategy. You are using the guaranteed income to enjoy your life. You know how much you'll get each month and how much will be left over. You can't do that with stocks or bonds. Those you let grow as you enjoy the annuity. When the annuity is gone, you've got a bigger pie of stocks and bonds. You can use some of that to . . . buy another annuity!

ACTION STEPS

- Accept that sometimes, in the long run, a smaller yet conservative return is much better than a risky yet larger return.
- Remember that even though it might have taken you years to build your castle, one strong tsunami can always wash it away.
- Don't follow the herd mentality. Do what's best for you and your family.
- Be patient and don't get greedy. Pigs get fed, but hogs get slaughtered.

PART IV

LEAVE IT!

REALITY CHECK

PROTECT YOUR MONEY
FROM DISABILITY
AND THE NURSING HOME.

MEET LINDA AND GARY

Linda and Gary were the classic greatest-generation couple—he was a veteran, she was a hardworking spouse. Gary gave her a blue-dyed carnation every Sunday, which she wore proudly to church. They lost their son, Peter, in his early 30s.

For Linda and Gary, money was in a way a reflection of the love and respect they had for each other. They weren't after money for fancy cars or vacations, but rather to ensure that they could take care of each other.

They were already well into their 70s when they became clients, so they required different treatment than 35-year-old millennials. For Linda and Gary, I designed a plan of bond ladders, which gave them varying amounts of income over time with no equity-market risk. I also assembled what I call a Preservation Portfolio, with conservative assets such as Treasury bills, so they knew they weren't going to lose any capital and could sleep at night. They were about 80 percent in fixed income and 20 percent in equities.

Gary passed away some years ago, but Linda had plenty of money available to retrofit their house so Gary could comfortably live out his days at home instead of in the nearby nursing home. Linda often tells me that she kept her promise to Gary, and that he died with dignity. That might be the most successful financial planning of all.

PLANNING STARTS WITH PLANNING FOR THE UNKNOWN

For many people, taking care of their family's expenses all the way to the grave via savings and investment income is the Holy Grail. But lots of people just can't manage this, or they have other things they'd rather spend their money on. For them, a mix of prudent investment and spend-down strategies, disability insurance, and long-term-care insurance may be the best way to go.

Let's look at the pros and cons of a few. . . .

We can start with the famous Aflac Duck. You've seen the commercials and may have wondered what all the quacking was about.

It's about disability insurance.

This is something almost nobody worries about, because they assume that they're covered at work. Perhaps surprisingly, I've found that doctors and dentists are among the most misinformed and underinsured in case they become disabled—because they already have it, but they are underinsured.

If you do have disability insurance from your workplace, and it's available, sign up now. If supplemental coverage is offered, buy that, too. Make sure you also compare your workplace plan's terms, conditions, and costs with a private disability plan.

If you don't have any coverage from work, consider the Aflac Duck or one of its competitors. Beware, though, that these plans, as helpful as they are, are only short-term, covering a part of your salary for a limited time if you're unable to work.

If you only have limited resources, scrap the duck and buy long-term disability coverage. A rule of thumb is to insure two-thirds of your income. An important point to remember is that most long-term disability policies cover your specific occupation. If you're a dentist and can't perform dentistry because of a hand ailment, you could still become, say, a financial advisor and earn income from that while collecting your disability benefits. It's perfectly legal, so long as you have an "Own Occupation" definition of disability. Avoid plans that have an "Any Occupation" definition of disability. With an "Any Occupation," if you can say the phrase "Welcome to Walmart," you *must* work at Walmart—even if you were a hand surgeon. No disrespect to Walmart workers. Furthermore, make sure your plan covers mental and nervous disorders as well as depression and anxiety. In an era where we are much more aware of mental health issues, its important you find a disability plan that covers those.

Many long-term plans have what they call a 90-day elimination period. Think of it like a deductible for car insurance—you have to pay the first $500, say, of any claim. On long-term disability, you may want to opt to self-insure for the first 90 days of care to keep the costs down on the policy. Make sure your plan lasts until you are at least 65 (ask if you can go up to 67 or 70 for an additional fee!), and make sure it's noncancelable and guaranteed renewable, which means the insurance company can't raise the rate every year and force you to cancel.

Here's something almost nobody thinks about. If you have working-age kids without disability coverage, what are they going to do if they are unable to perform their occupation due to a heart attack, stroke, or cancer? They're going to come live with you, that's what! So protect everybody by giving them a gift of disability insurance. It would make a great Christmas, Hanukkah, or graduation gift.

Once you've got your regular coverage and short- and long-term disability covered, you can start thinking about long-term care.

How important is this?

As surely as you will get older, especially if you are blessed with good health, suddenly the risk will be not longevity, but end-of-life care. There are a lot of surveys out there showing how much medical care costs as we get older. Most of them estimate about $300,000 per person for a 60-year-old. Add in a high inflation rate for drugs and medical care, and dental and vision care, and it easily becomes on average $500,000 per person. You'll need savings for part of this, but you really, really need insurance that's going to cover you at the end of your life. Who would you rather have all of your life savings go to when you pass: people you love, or the nursing home?

MEDICARE AND ITS PARTS

Let's look at Medicare first. This government plan currently covers about 44 million Americans over the age of 65, a number expected to rise to 79 million by 2030 as the trailing group of baby boomers reaches retirement age.

It consists of Part A, which covers hospitalization and nursing care. It's free, but there is a yearly deductible and copayment on many services. You're automatically signed up when you reach age 65. Part A usually covers about 80 percent of billed expenses.

Part B covers doctor visits and some medical supplies. Most people sign up when they're enrolled in Part A. There's a monthly premium for Part B, which rises with income level.

Part C is either a Medicare Advantage or Medicare Supplement plan, which are available for a monthly fee from many insurers. There are many flavors of these plans, and you should read all the fine print before you buy the one that suits you best.

Part D is the prescription drug plan, and it's often one of the most important things you can buy. There's a monthly premium, but most plans cover the majority of the medicines you're ever going to need, often for no extra charge to you when you get them in the mail or from your neighborhood drugstore.

You are probably going to want to make sure you and your spouse are signed up for all four parts.

MEDICAID

Many people think Medicaid is a program that gives health insurance to poor people with little income who otherwise couldn't afford insurance. And it is. But few people realize that Medicaid is also the biggest provider of coverage for people in nursing homes. Medicaid covers most of the 1.4 million Americans in nursing homes, which consumes more than 40 percent of the program's budget.

For older people with no assets, it's the difference between dignity and cat food. But for people with some assets, there's a problem. You don't have enough money to pay for the nursing home yourself, but you've got too much money to qualify for Medicaid. For millions of people, this is a real problem.

MEET MARTHA

Martha came to see me right after her husband passed away. He was 71 and had just retired from his job selling insurance. She was also 71 and had never handled any of the family's finances. Harry had done all that.

And not that badly. She had $100,000 to her name, including a $60,000 check Harry had received from an insurance settlement before he died.

She herself was in shaky health and knew she didn't want to just give all her money to the government or to a nursing home when she got sick. Her kids and grandkids were great but had money worries of their own, what with Jason needing a new roof and Carol needing a new car and all those grandkids to put through college one day. Because the house was all paid up and she had no mortgage payments, Martha was frugal enough to get by on Social Security, hers and Harry's, and a little from savings.

My meeting with Martha was one of the most touching of my career. This dear woman relied on me for her plans. Martha's biggest fear involved her osteoporosis and hunched back. She worried about needing to go into a nursing home in maybe 10 years, which she knew she couldn't afford. Harry never bothered with long-term-care insurance. She's going to need to depend on Medicaid for the nursing coverage.

But as we've seen, Medicaid basically requires that you have no assets, and haven't had any for the previous five years. That's known as the Medicaid Look-Back. She'd need to spend that $100,000 and be destitute before Medicaid would pay for the nursing home. She really didn't want to get caught in the Medicaid spend-down trap.

I advised her to write four checks of $15,000 each to her children and grandchildren, and to have all of them put the money into stock fund accounts and didn't touch it. Since these were proceeds from Harry's settlement check, nobody owed any tax.

She'll easily get by until she needs the nursing home. So long as nothing bad happens to her within the next five years, she won't be a victim of the five-year look-back. Then, if something develops later on with her osteoporosis, she doesn't have to touch that $60,000 and can still go to a Medicaid facility.

LONG-TERM-CARE INSURANCE

Which brings us to a topic almost as fiercely debated as annuities: long-term-care insurance. There are five major objections to this type of insurance, so let's go through them.

1. **Medicare is going to take care of me.**
   No, it's not. Medicare doesn't cover nursing-home or hospice care. Such care can cost $250 a day or more, or about $100,000 a year. The average stay is three years, so $300,000. If you're lucky and live for 20 years, that's $2 million.

2. **It's too expensive.**
   Not really. There are plans with premiums of a couple thousand dollars a year and others far more reasonable than paying $100,000 a year for three years of coverage in a nursing home. It's probably best to buy these plans in your late 40s or 50s, but they are also available for people in their 60s and 70s.

3. **The insurers are all collapsing under the weight of too many claims and are raising rates out of sight.**
   There have been a few cases of insurers in trouble who have been forced to either go out of business (still, they

have been taken over by the state) or raise rates. There are still some insurance companies that have managed to mainly hold the line on rates.

4. **Why pay all these premiums when I might not need it for 30 years and maybe never?**
    Insurance depends on a pool of people paying in premiums and using benefits when they need them. Nobody can be sure they're never going to get sick. If you're roaring healthy in your 80s, you should feel fortunate. The best policy may be the one you don't have to use. However, if you or your spouse do fall ill, you're going to be grateful you bought this coverage.

5. **Won't Medicaid cover my long-term care even if Medicare won't?**
    Yes, but at a cost you're probably not willing to pay. Medicaid does provide care for many nursing-home patients, but that care can be pretty basic, and you have to have essentially no income and spend down your assets to only $2,000 in order to qualify. It's a program for poor people, not your basic retiree. Some people do try to spend down all their assets so they qualify, but there are far better solutions, such as long-term-care insurance.

    Long-term-care insurance, like annuities, has gotten terrible press. That's partly because it can be expensive, especially if you buy it when you're 70 instead of 60. But think of what's better: to spend approximately $2,500 for 20 years on a policy or to lose $100,000 a year due to end-of-life care. On top of that, many policies give you the ability to stay at home or get assisted living, not just reside in a nursing home.

MEET GERALD AND EVE

Gerald is now 87. When he was 77, we bought him a long-term-care policy from Allianz, the giant German insurer world-renowned for its solid stewardship of money. It was all good until this year, when Allianz told its policyholders it was going to raise premiums by 10 percent each of the next three years, after a decade of no increases.

Gerald panicked. He wanted to drop the policy.

Wrong! All health-care insurance tends to go up with inflation, and he needed to be reminded that they didn't raise his rate for 10 years. A 30 percent increase over 10 years is equal to about a 3 percent inflation. The policy was still sound, and Gerald and Eve are ever closer to needing the Cadillac benefits they've been paying for. Besides, he was paying $2,000 a year, which would be $2,600, even after the increase in premiums. For comparison's sake, $2,600 is a good price now for a 62-year-old looking at long-term-care insurance.

We kept the policy.

If you've already got a long-term-care policy, keep it. If you don't have one, consider buying one, no matter how old you are. If you want to stay in your own home and hire nursing care rather than go into a nursing home, buy a policy with an in-home care rider. It may be a little more expensive, but it's worth it if that's what you want.

ACTION STEPS

- Proper health-care planning involves a mix of Medicare, Medicare supplements, and other private insurance such as long-term care.
- No one can predict health crises, so the more flexible and available the coverage, the better.
- Find an advisor that makes plans easily understandable to spouses and children.
- Run right now and get a Durable Power of Attorney, Health Care Directives, and Living Will, to make sure your wishes are respected.

15

REALITY CHECK

ESTATE PLANNING:
WHAT IS THAT?

MEET RYAN

Ryan is a multimillionaire, but the story of how he organized his estate is applicable to virtually anyone.

He made a substantial income trading bonds for a big multinational investment firm and came to us seeking advice on how to best leave all that money to his grown daughters, Jill and Jane, without the US government taking most of it, and in a way that the daughters (who loved each other, but money is money) wouldn't be able to fight over it.

We bought him two very large life insurance policies, one on each of his daughters. But we did it with a twist, so these policies ended up acting like trusts.

Jane is the owner of her sister Jill's policy, and Jill owns Jane's policy. That way, while Jane—if she wanted—could ruin Jill, Jill could ruin Jane! It was like mutually assured destruction. They've got to work together!

The proceeds of the life insurance death benefit will go to the daughters' income and estate tax-free and creditor-proof.

Ryan's story is just one example of estate planning.

Relax. Estate planning may sound boring and complicated and only something yacht-wielding billionaires with teams of accountants indulge in over the odd mint julep.

Nope.

Estate planning just means getting your act together in plenty of time before you die so that your money goes exactly where you want it to go.

I know—you're not going to be around, so what does it matter?

It matters a lot to those people and philanthropic causes you love and devote your life to. And it's so painless and easy that it's truly a shame that everybody doesn't take care of this when they can.

Estate planning is a holistic process. Many advisors think it's just a matter of setting up some trusts, paying the lawyers' fees, and forgetting about it for 30 years.

But to do it right, you've also got to look at your total net worth. If it's more than a couple of hundred thousand, you're going to want to explore trusts, lawyers' fees notwithstanding. (Transfer on death accounts and life insurance might do the same job.) You've also got to look at your health insurance, especially long-term care, which isn't going to be covered by Medicare. Estate-planning decisions depend not only on your situation and hopes and dreams, but also may depend on where you live. Each state's laws are different.

Estate planning is mostly a matter of gathering the right documents and putting them in the care of somebody you trust who's going to outlive you.

WHAT ARE THOSE DOCUMENTS?

1. You need a will. If you do not have a will, get one. You can get it done by a lawyer if you know one, or on one of many websites. Google "I need a will" and take your pick. Your will names an executor and instructs that executor about matters such as paying for your funeral and how and to whom you want to leave your assets. Normally a married couple first leaves assets to the surviving spouse. Complicated estates may include things like charitable trusts and other tax-reduction items.

2. You need a living will, one of the great misnamed documents. A living will is really just instructions to your loved and trusted people about how you want to handle the last part of your life. This may include a Do Not Resuscitate Order if you don't want extraordinary measures taken to prolong your life—if you fall into a coma, for example.

3. You need a revocable trust. This is an invaluable estate-planning document; because it can be revoked, you have full control, and it bypasses probate in states where probate can be a real problem. Even in states where probate isn't costly, it may be valuable if you want your estate private, as a will is a matter of public record. Most people don't realize that.

There are other trusts that come into play for larger estates. One is the so-called dynasty trust that lets you avoid estate tax for a set number of years. In a couple of states, that period can be forever. It's also better to set up this sort of trust in states with no state income or estate tax, such as South Dakota, Nevada, Alaska, or Wyoming.

Keep in mind that it's irrevocable; so once the assets are in the trust, your trustee needs to dole out the money. However, some can be changed due to decanting provisions.

If you've got a lot of assets, it's worth talking to your advisor about one of these trusts. In most cases, they can be domiciled anywhere, not just in the state where you live. Rhode Island, surprisingly, protects your assets in the event of a divorce and against spouse or child support. It's important to find a state where your assets are protected against the unexpected. Let's say you want to leave money to your daughter, a successful executive, who marries a real loser. He turns around and divorces her and sues for child support. In some states, including Delaware and Ohio, her inheritance from you might be in jeopardy.

If you want to get more exotic, and aggressive, about protecting your assets in a trust, various island nations offer all sorts of options. Bermuda, the Bahamas, and the Cayman Islands offer protection that's real, if sometimes abused. Just make sure you declare it on your income taxes and apply with FATCA reporting.

There's even something called the Cook Islands Trust, used by, among others, Mitt Romney. This is a strategy for rich people. Money located overseas, in tax havens like the Cook Islands, grows tax-free. Sometimes it's a good idea to make the beneficiary of your life insurance policy such a trust. You've got to pay taxes when you bring it back to the US, or it is inherited, but there are also good, legal strategies to minimize this taxation. You must report it, but tax can be deferred using some of the strategies we've already discussed.

This is by no means an exhaustive list. It's just a prod. Talk to your advisor about your family situation and anything you worry about. They need to worry about it, too.

In addition to the three estate-planning documents presented above, if you own a business or property, you need the deeds or ownership agreements. Collect them all up, or have your accountant or attorney do so, and put them in the same safe place you've got your will. If there's been any legal correspondence about this stuff, put that in there, too. Also, consider a buy-sell agreement, which ensures your heirs are bought out of the business if you die with sufficient insurance.

And finally, for all the documents mentioned, put them all in a safe place. Put copies of any insurance policies (the stuff you may have tossed out) in there as well. We recommend a handy binder to our clients with special tabs for your estate planning documents, income plan, investment statements, and other essential financial documents.

Once you've got everything assembled, show it all to your advisor and start having the Estate Planning Conversation.

ACTION STEPS

- Assemble your key documents, including your last will and testament, living will, and any ongoing business agreements.
- Consult with your advisor regularly to update your wishes and documents.
- Explore many options for estate planning. Even those that seem exotic may save you money.
- Go to retirementrealitycheck.com, enter code BINDER, and after an initial consultation, you can purchase our estate planning binder for a low price of $19.99.

CONCLUSION

WINNING THE GAME

MEET DAVID AND JANET

David is a retired journalist who never paid attention to the 4 percent rule—or any other financial rule, for that matter.

By faithfully maxing out his IRA contributions and amassing whatever stock options he was offered by his company, he managed to cobble together a retirement fund of $2 million, mostly in a tax-deferred IRA.

His advisors crafted a Monte Carlo analysis showing he had enough money to retire, which David promptly put in a drawer and ignored. They also gave him a spending plan, which he likewise ignored, and a Social Security maximization strategy, which he followed.

David and his wife, Janet, retired to his native Chicago after living in London, Paris, Hong Kong, and New Jersey. They like to go to performances of the Chicago Symphony, the Lyric Opera, and the Goodman Theater; they go to lots of Chicago Cubs games, and they happily support the Chicago Art Institute, the Field Museum of Natural History, the Shedd Aquarium, and the Chicago Council on Global Affairs. They both volunteer at a local food pantry and donate generously.

David pretty much did everything we've talked about in this book. His advisors had him nicely diversified in stock and bond funds and even put $200,000 in a little-known fund that invested mainly in things like dry cleaners and returned a healthy rate of return before cashing out.

David had a life insurance policy that protected his earnings while he was working, and both he and Janet have long-term-care policies with home-care riders that will allow them to end their days at home if they so choose. They're both on Medicare and have supplemental policies as well as Part D drug coverage and dental insurance.

David has never watched CNBC and isn't about to start. He'd rather watch baseball.

MEET JOSH

Yeah, it's me.

I said early on that I have used all the strategies that I recommend in this book, and I have.

After getting out of our $60,000 credit-card debt, my wife and I put away whatever we could while still maintaining date nights in our pre-kids phase and yearly vacations, even after we've had five (soon to be six) kids! These helped make all that saving worthwhile.

As soon as I could financially, I bought both term life insurance to cover my income and cash-value life insurance to start building a volatility buffer. As my income picked up, I stored away as much as I could into a dividend-paying participating permanent life insurance policy ($44,000 per year by the age of 28!). Then I used the volatility buffer the insurance afforded me to invest in the stock market without much regard to the risks associated.

I've put money away for the kids' college, and we've got life insurance with an accelerated death benefit for long-term care, so they're not going to have to worry about us and we're not going to have to worry about Medicaid spend-downs. I know our stock, ETFs, and mutual funds are going to decline in value at some point, and I also know they're going to come back up after a while. I don't intend to touch them for a while.

As I grew up, I was the kid with the lemonade stand, the newspaper route. I weeded people's yards for money. I cut people's lawns. I would save up because my parents didn't have any money for my Super Mario Brothers video games. I learned the value of a dollar, and from the age of five I read about all matters financial.

My dad and I would look at the newspaper stock tables and circle what stocks we thought would go up. Think Alex P. Keaton in *Family Ties*. I read books by Larry Burkett. I was highly into buying everything with cash, avoiding debt, and not buying stupid stuff.

My parents didn't really avoid buying stupid stuff. They weren't extravagant, but they did put trips to Disney World on their credit cards. They didn't pay much attention to insurance. My dad was never encouraged to buy disability insurance from his financial advisor. In fact, my dad probably didn't have enough money to even be considered a client of a financial advisor. When my dad worked at a bank in the 1990s, he (and virtually everyone else) saw their guaranteed pensions turned into 401(k)s that supposedly would give everyone a chance to secure their own retirement. The idea was that you didn't need a pension because in 20 or 30 years you'd have a million dollars due to the stock market's growth, and if you did that you didn't need things like permanent life insurance or annuities. They didn't buy them.

My dad was all excited about rolling his pension over into the 401(k). He was thrilled with a year or two of gains in the 1990s, and then a string of disabilities without disability insurance forced him to liquidate his 401(k) to pay the mortgage and make ends meet for our family. He did what everybody said to do—buy term insurance and invest the difference. He cashed out his whole-life policy for a cheaper term policy, but the term policy wasn't convertible to a good whole life, so when his term expired, he was left without any insurance.

At age 11, I got a call that my 40-year-old father had had a heart attack and was going to St. Peter's Hospital in Jersey City for an angioplasty balloon surgery. For 30-some years I lived with the keen awareness that my father might die. (He died last year.) That had a profound impact on me.

When I got the call, I remember worrying, "Will he make it? Will he live to see my kids? Will he make it to my wedding?"

Even at that early age, I decided I was going to do what my parents hadn't done. I was going to pay attention to safety and protection, not just money. I have tried to live my life on this basis. I got scholarships, paid my way through college, and graduated debt-free. I sometimes told my mother, "I learned what not to do by watching you, and what to do," and that financial planning should be about what you enjoy, not just what you save

Because I have always wanted to help the poor, I moved into inner-city Philadelphia, got a master's degree in divinity, and put my financial passion on hold for a little bit to see how I could serve people in a deeper way. I went on mission trips and worked as a night watchman for the Advanta Credit Card Company and the Wellington Fund, thinking maybe I wanted to develop my financial career. For a time, I did pastoral work at a Korean Presbyterian church, an Episcopal church, and a nondenominational one.

In Philadelphia I met Pastor Bill Devlin, a magnetic personality to whom I owe a lot of my orientation and dedication. Pastor Bill taught me that, even if you want to help people, and even if you're a pastor, money becomes a necessity. No matter what you do, he said, even if you're Mother Teresa, "You still gotta eat and your flock still gotta eat."

I found myself begging for bread just to serve people. And as I was in that new endeavor, I was getting into grad-school debt, and even though I was serving people and not doing it for money, that money began to have a greater hold on me than I'd ever realized. *I wanted eventually to have the financial freedom to do what I love.*

I threw myself headlong into a financial modeling software that I still use to this day called Wealth in Motion™. It teaches that math isn't money and money isn't math, an idea promoted by Bob Castiglione, author of the book *LEAP: Lifetime Economic Acceleration Process*. Life often doesn't work out according to our financial plan, mainly because of what are known as "wealth-eroding factors." These factors include taxes, inflation, investment fees, planned obsolescence, disability, life events, and market fluctuations.

You can't base your life on "oh, I hope the market will go up." Or "oh, I hope I never have a disability," or "oh, I hope I don't die early." Hope should never be the basis of your financial plan.

Maybe you'll never attain the mythic retirement you dream of. But you should enjoy your days on this earth. You should have memories with your kids and grandkids. Maybe you don't have to retire at 62. Maybe you want to take a vacation every year in your 30s and 40s and retire at 70.

This book gives you options.

When I read *Rich Dad Poor Dad* by Robert Kiyosaki, I started thinking that I could buy assets that would produce income to give me a measure of freedom.

I realized that debt is enslavement. And if you don't know how to wisely use money as an entrepreneur or as an investor, you can easily become enslaved to it. If you don't use money as a tool, money will become your master.

You don't want that. You want to be in a position of freedom to serve, to bless, to enjoy.

I don't believe *any* financial product is going to make anybody rich.

These products—exchange-traded funds, annuities, whole-life insurance, whatever—are really just places to store money to offset the effects of inflation and wealth-eroding factors, such as a stock-market decline, personal disability, early death of you or your spouse, and something nobody thinks about until it's too late, planned obsolescence risk—your refrigerator is definitely going to break before you expect it to.

You're not going to get rich protecting yourself from all these risks, but that's the heart of financial planning, and it's going to let you sleep a lot better.

TAKEAWAYS

What I hope you'll take away from these stories and this book is that, with a little unconventional thinking and a lot of thought and planning, retirement can be a pleasure, not an ordeal.

First, you've got to shuck off all that dreary advice about giving up lattes in order to pay down credit-card debt and selling off your whole-life policies, buying a term policy and investing the difference in premiums, or only ever taking 4 percent a year out of your retirement savings. That's old, tired advice geared to the way things used to work 60 years ago.

Once you've done that, you can build up a volatility buffer, diversify your investments properly, develop a bunch of extra revenue streams, organize your affairs to pay the legal minimum in taxes, plan your estate so you leave what you want to whom you want, and still have enough to tend to the health needs of yourself and your spouse as you get older.

Along the way, you should have enough cash to live comfortably, travel, eat out, pursue a hobby, and give time and money to charities you care about, without ever having to worry about the Dow Jones Industrial Average on any given day.

Remember the Old Reality and New Reality lists from Reality Check One? (See pages 9 and 10.) If you can manage to turn a blind eye to the accepted wisdom in the first list and adopt the recommendations in the second list, you'll be well on your way to a joyful retirement.

Again, this is a holistic approach. All the pieces work together to help you enjoy the money you've worked so hard for. It lets you do what you want to do, not what somebody else thinks you're supposed to do.

You've now got all the tools to enjoy your retirement.

God's blessings on your health and your wealth.

ACTION STEPS

- If you don't have an investment advisor, get one.
- Be open and vocal with your advisor about your economic situation, prospects, and dreams.
- Reject conventional wisdom and think differently. Your future depends on it.
- If you skipped some chapters of this book, that's okay. They'll still be here if and when you need them.
- Enjoy your money. You never know how long you have!

ACKNOWLEDGMENTS

I want to thank:

Mommy—my heart aches that the woman whom I danced with to "You Raise Me Up" at my wedding is no longer on this earth. I miss your hugs and your unconditional love. I am forever indebted to the Lord for the love of the best mom in the world.

Daddy—the day I had been dreading for 30 years came true last year. I lost my biggest fan, my most avid listener, and the greatest dad in all the world. Your death was my fear as a kid, my fuel as an adult, and I hope that someday my kids will think I'm as great as you and Mom. I'm glad I will see you and Mom again—because He lives.

Bethie—my heart, the only love of my life, you are fiercely loyal, my greatest muse, the most tender mother, and the dearest friend. The loveliest beauty in all the universe. I married up and will spend my days praising the Lord for allowing me the privilege of being married to someone I don't deserve. "A wife of noble character who can find? She is worth far more than rubies."

Elisabeth (wise and kind), Marilyn (smart and sweet), Josh (congenial and intelligent), Judah (discerning and a leader), Moses (healing and loving), and baby due just as this book comes out—I am so blessed to have the most beautiful, smart, strong, and kind kids, who are a testament to the Lord and their mommy.

Sweet baby Grace. The day you were born was the happiest and saddest day of my life. At least we met once. Looking forward to seeing you in eternity.

Bill (never misses a show), Tina (always there for me), and Jessica (through the years you never let me down)—the most loving siblings in all the world.

My mother-in-love and father-in-love, Bet and Mike. So glad I have in-laws who love so deeply.

Matt, Nini, Popi, and all my family in heaven looking down on us.

I am indebted to Phil Revzin for his significant help with turning conversations on the car ride home into a real book. Complete thanks to Steve Blumenthal, John Mauldin, Larry Kotlikoff, Sara Kendrick (my patient and tireless editor), Jeff Farr (my other longsuffering editor), Beth Metrick (production), Matthew Bomberger (best graphic designer I know), the folks at HarperCollins Leadership, Barry Dyke, and Tim Burgard for taking a chance on me.

Without the experiences and support from my clients and staff family at Jalinski Advisory Group, Inc., and Wealth Quarterback, LLC, this book would not exist. You are family and loved and appreciated. Thank you to Jim, Shelly, Lori (my first real employee), Michele, Elaine, David, Nicolette, Rich, Carl, JoAnn, Tina, Tyler, and Jess. My CPA, Tony. My pastor, Bill, who comes late to the hospital when our kids are born . . . and when our sweet baby was born asleep.

Megan Close Zavala, for believing in the book from the start. Wendy Keller, whose personal story inspired me to finish this project amid the greatest loss of my life. She is equally inspiring as an agent.

I want to thank my Lord and Savior Jesus Christ, most of all, because money isn't the purpose of life . . . God is.

NOTES

Reality Check One
1. https://news.feinberg.northwestern.edu/2018/04/financial-losses -linked-to-greater-risk-of-death/.

Reality Check Two
1. Such plans typically incur set-up fees, annual administration fees, and investment management fees.
2. At 2019 annual contribution limits.
3. But not more than the cash value of the policy.

Reality Check Three
1. Suze Orman, *The Money Book for the Young, Fabulous & Broke* (New York: Riverhead Books, 2005).
2. https://www.bloomberg.com/news/articles/2016-05-10/comcast-pays -490-million-to-settle-ralph-roberts-life-insurance.
3. https://www.youtube.com/watch?v=XTXbiWcaL1M.
4. http://www.equiasalliance.com/images/PDFs/boli-holdings-reports /Q4-2017-BOLI-Holdings-Report.pdf.
5. https://www.thinkadvisor.com/2017/08/18/your-5-best-arguments -for-life-insurance-besides-t/.

Reality Check Four
1. https://www.thinkadvisor.com/2016/02/23/the-annuity-99-of-clients -should-avoid-and-one-tha/.
2. https://states.aarp.org/a-secure-choice-for-savings/.

Reality Check Seven

1. https://www.bankonyourself.com/bank-on-yourself-insurance-companies.

Reality Check Ten

1. https://awealthofcommonsense.com/2018/10/a-lost-decade-of-dollar -cost-averaging/.
2. https://personal.vanguard.com/pdf/s315.pdf.
3. https://awealthofcommonsense.com/2018/10/a-lost-decade-of-dollar -cost-averaging/.

INDEX